LIVERPOOL PRINTED TILES
BY
ANTHONY RAY

Contents

© Anthony Ray 1994
Produced and designed by
Jonathan Horne Publications
66c Kensington Church Street
London W8 4BY
ISBN 0 9512140 7 1

FRONT COVER

A3-1	A5-3	A2-1	A1-1
B4-9	B4-2	B1-1	B3-11
D6-3	B9-4	D1-1	B5-2
D8-32	D8-35	D8-12	D8-26
F1-17	F1-15	F1-5	F1-7

Acknowledgements

Monnie Kanter, the well known Chicago surgeon, was the instigator of this publication. He has been a keen collector of Liverpool transfer printed tiles for the past 25 years, but with the thought of retirement not too far away and the possibility of moving to a smaller house, he decided to sell to me his entire collection of over 140 different subjects. Consequently, it was decided to produce a catalogue as a means of promoting what was probably the largest collection of printed tiles in private hands. On further reflection, it was felt that in this form it would only be half a catalogue, and that the opportunity should not be missed to publish all the known printed subjects, of which over 370 have now been recorded. Who else was there to turn to but Anthony Ray, who has done so much work on this subject. His co-operation has now made this production viable.

Sincere thanks go to Audrey Atterbury, The Detroit Institute of Arts (*F2-6*), Mr. and Mrs. Guy Jones and The Wedgwood Museum for supplying material; and also to Michael Archer, David Drakard, Pat Halfpenny, Bonita LaMarche, Gaye Blake-Roberts, Norman Stretton, Dr. Bernard Watney, and many others who have helped and advised in this project.

J.K.H. June 1994

Author's Preface

Almost a century has passed since John Hodgkin, that remarkable student and collector of English delftware tiles, published his pioneering articles on John Sadler in the Burlington Magazine, including the first attempt at a catalogue of printed tiles. These articles remained for many years the standard work on the subject, but while collecting material for *English Delftware Tiles*, I soon realised that Hodgkin's catalogue was far from complete. With the help of private collectors and of friends in museums it did not take long to record a total of 312 designs, very nearly twice the number in Hodgkin's lists. These were published as a fully illustrated catalogue in the *Transactions of the English Ceramic Circle* in 1973, accompanied by a transcript of the paper read to the Circle in November 1972, whose aim was to discuss particular problems connected with the tiles rather than provide a purely historical overview. Since then friends have brought to my notice a number of previously unrecorded designs, and these too have been published in various volumes of the *Transactions*, bringing the catalogue up to date and swelling the number of designs to around 370. Bernard Watney and others have published unrecorded design sources and much work has been done recently on Sadler's printing methods. The original text has therefore been considerably revised, to incorporate and discuss this new material and to present a more coherent historical account of what was a very remarkable enterprise.

I am very grateful to Jonathan Horne for the opportunity to bring the earlier work up to date, and to the President and Committee of the English Ceramic Circle for giving their blessing to this project. Finally I should like to express my thanks not only to those mentioned in Jonathan Horne's foreword, but also to all those who over the years have helped me in my studies.

A.R.

JOHN SADLER AND GUY GREEN

In the second half of the 18th century Liverpool was a very busy pottery centre, especially for the manufacture of delftware and porcelain; indeed it had, after Staffordshire, the largest concentration of potters in England, and it carried on a thriving export trade. Among other things it made tiles which are among the finest in the history of tile-making, and it was there that the first transfer-printed tiles were produced, in the mid-1750's.

In fact it was not a potter who saw that the very recent developments in the art of printing on fired materials, such as porcelain, glass and enamels, could be applied to tiles, but John Sadler, a man trained as a printer. Born at Aintree in 1720, he was the son of Adam Sadler who, according to Mayer, the Liverpool historian, acquired an interest in printing as a soldier during Marlborough's campaigns in the Low Countries when he was billeted on a printer. At all events he apparently left the army soon after and set himself up as a printer in Liverpool. John Sadler followed in his father's footsteps, his earliest recorded work being the pamphlet *A Short Account of a Course of Philosophy and Astronomy* by J.Arden of Derby, published from an unknown address. In 1748 he purchased from his father a house in Harrington Street which from then on remained his centre of operations. As a publisher he seems to have produced mainly devotional and studious works, including a Latin grammar, but his most considerable achievements in this field were *The Muses' Delight (1) of 1754,* and *The Liverpool Chronicle and Marine Gazette, 1757.* It is not known exactly when he began his experiments with printing on tiles (2), but commercial production did not begin until 1756-7. In the following years he also printed enamels and porcelain (3) but his association with Wedgwood, which began in 1761, meant that he had to concentrate on printing creamware and tiles. By 1766 he was, on his own admission, becoming tired of business and sold all his printing presses, while retaining an interest in the printed tiles, and in 1770 he could afford to retire, handing over the business to Guy Green. In 1777 he married and the union produced a daughter in 1782. Sadler died in 1789 and it was from this daughter that Mayer obtained information about her father and, most importantly, the documents relating to a possible patent and Sadler's note-book.

The date 1766 is inscribed on the cover of the note-book, the first entry being made on 1 January 1766, and Sadler continued adding notes until 15 January 1788 (4). In spite of being in a somewhat chaotic state, with many erasures and with the pages in no certain chronological order, it is a precious document which says something about his life, since personal expenses are included, but far more about his interest in recipes, not just those which would be of use to his business as a tile-printer, which will be referred to later, but also others which have a domestic or medical purpose. He emerges as a man with an enquiring spirit, and also as someone fond of good living who shared the general enthusiasm of the time for punch-parties. He also had a passion for music and organised concerts in Liverpool.

The other source of information about John Sadler is his correspondence with Wedgwood, though this naturally tells us more about his activities as a businessman. It is obvious that much of the success of Sadler's enterprise was due to Guy Green, who had also been apprenticed to Adam Sadler as a printer. The Affidavit and Certificate both bear Green's signature and, had the petition for a patent been successful, he would certainly have been a beneficiary. This suggests that he was at an early date in some kind of association with Sadler, although the legal partnership dates from 1761 when Sadler undertook to print Wedgwood's creamware as well as tiles. After Sadler's retirement in 1770 Guy Green continued to run the establishment, continuing to print tiles until at least 1780, after which date his activities are not documented; it is possible that like many others he turned to dealing in pottery (5). The term 'Sadler tiles', therefore, is used here, as elsewhere, only for convenience. The only printed delftware tiles of the eighteenth century, apart from those made by their apprentice Richard Abbey, they might all justifiably be called 'Sadler and Green' tiles.

Finally it is important to stress that neither John Sadler nor Guy Green had any training as potters and they must have had considerable practical help from the Liverpool delftware potters, notably Samuel Gilbody and Thomas Shaw, who signed the Certificate. The invention of printing on tiles was clearly a co-operative effort drawing on the skills and talents of many people.

---

1. For the frontispiece see WATNEY, 1966, pl. 60b
2. It cannot have been before Brooks' patent of 1751, and it is unlikely to have preceded Brooks' patent of 1753. A date c.1755 seems most likely.
3. Of 1758 are the enamelled Grand Bucks and Masons medals, together with a snuff-box enamelled with a complete Almanac for 1759, and a portrait medallion of Frederick III (actually Frederick II), King of Prussia. Of 1759 is the snuff-box with a Ladies' Pocket Kalendar (sic). Another portrait of Frederick and one of George II may date from 1760. After this date he appears to have given up printing on enamels, though he continued to print porcelain.
4. The entries after 1770 were clearly intended to assist Guy Green.
5. Gore's directories from 1781 to 1803 mostly refer to him as a China Manufacturer, though that of 1790 calls the Harrington Street premises a 'China Painter's Shop' and that of 1796 a 'Printed China Warehouse'.

JOHN SADLER AND THE LIVERPOOL TILE INDUSTRY

In the scanty literature on English tiles there is a natural tendency to treat the printed tiles separately from the painted tiles, but it is with the Liverpool painted tiles that one must begin, for reasons which will quickly become apparent. As is well known, the earliest document referring to the manufacture of delftware in Liverpool is the announcement in the *Liverpool Post Boy* for 23 May 1710:

"The corporation of Liverpool in Lancashire have encouraged there a manufactory of all sorts of fine and painted pots and other vessels and tiles in imitation of China both for Inland and Outland trade, which will be speedily ready and sold at reasonable prices."

The mention of tiles is important, and since the potters who came to Liverpool were recruited in London it is most probable that they made 'London tiles', which at this period were certainly very Dutch in character - with landscapes, scenes from the Bible, flower-vases and so on, in blue or manganese monochrome. It is impossible to say anything about the earliest Liverpool tiles or attribute specimens to the Liverpool potteries, but by the middle of the century a more readily identifiable Liverpool tile seems to have evolved, still Dutch in character, but, like other English tiles of the 1740s, with native characteristics. A further point of importance is that the Dutch potters were exporting large quantities of tiles to England at this time, and that Liverpool was an important outlet for them. There are two pieces of evidence to support this assumption. The first is that many Liverpool tiles of the period 1750-70 imitate or copy Dutch originals. The strong commercial instincts of the thriving Liverpool pottery trade had been aroused, and the potters seemed to have answered the Dutch challenge, firstly by making these imitations and then by developing the polychrome tile which was virtually unknown in Holland at this time. The second piece of evidence is the wording of the Sadler documents, where Shaw and Gilbody state that one of the great advantages of Sadler's process was that "...the Dutch (who import large quantities of tiles into England, Ireland, etc.) may by this improvement be considerably undersold..."

The *Affidavit* and *Certificate* throw much light on the tile industry in Liverpool at this time and provide an essential date for the beginning of Sadler's enterprise, for which reason they are quoted here in full.

The Affidavit ———

I, John Sadler, Of Liverpoole, in the county of Lancaster, printer, and Guy Green of Liverpoole aforesaid, printer, severally maketh oath, that on Tuesday the 27th day of July instant, they these deponents, without the aid or assistance of any other person or persons, did within the space of six hours, to wit betwixt the hours of nine in the morning and three in the afternoon of the same day, print upwards of twelve hundred earthenware tiles of different patterns, at Liverpoole aforesaid, and which, as these deponents have heard and believe were more in number, and better, and neater than one hundred skilful pot painters could have painted in the like space of time in the common and usual way of painting with a pencil; and these deponents say that they have been upwards of seven years in finding out the method of printing tiles, and in making tryals and experiments for that purpose, which they have now, through great pains and expense, brought to perfection.

John Sadler
Guy Green

Taken and sworn at Liverpoole, in the county of Lancaster, the second day of August, one thousand and seven hundred and fifty-six before William Statham, a Master Extraordinary in Chancery.

The Certificate ———

We, Alderman Thomas Shaw and Samuel Gilbody, both of Liverpool, in the county of Lancaster, clay potters, whose names are hereto subscribed, do hereby humbly certifye that we are well assured that John Sadler and Guy Green did, at Liverpool aforesaid, on Tuesday, the 27th day of July last past, within the space of six hours, print upwards of 1200 earthenware tiles of different colours and patterns, which is, upon a moderate computation, more than 100 good workmen could have done of the same patterns in the same space of time by the usual way of painting with a pencil. That we have since burnt the above tiles, and that they are considerably neater than we have seen pencilled, and may be sold at little more than half the price. We are also assured that the said John Sadler and Guy Green have been several years in bringing the art of printing on earthenware to perfection, and we never heard it was done by any other person or persons but themselves. We are also assured that as the Dutch (who import large quantities of tiles into England, Ireland, etc) may by this improvement be considerably undersold, it cannot fail to be of great advantage to the nation, and to the towne of Liverpoole in particular, where the earthenware manufacture is more extensively carried out than in any other town in the Kingdom, and for which reasons we hope, and do not doubt, the above persons will be indulged in their request for a patent to secure to them the profits that may arise from the above useful and advantageous improvements.

Liverpoole, Aug. 13, 1756

To Charles Pole, Esq, in London

Sir,

John Sadler, the bearer, and Guy Green, both of this town, have invented a method of printing potters earthenware tyles for chimneys with surprising expedition. We have seen several of their printed tyles, and are of the opinion that they are superior to any done by the pencil, and that this invention will be highly advantageous to the Kingdom in general, and to the town of Liverpoole, in particular.

In consequence of which, and for the encouragement of so useful and ingenious an improvement, we desire the favour of your interest in procuring for them his Majesty's letters patent.

Ellis Cunliffe
Spencer Steers,
Charles Gore.

JOHN SADLER AND THE INVENTION OF
TRANSFER - PRINTING ON POTTERY

The claim that they had spent 'upwards of seven years' experimenting was evidently made more to give weight to their application for a patent rather than out of a statement of fact; otherwise they might be considered the inventors of transfer-printing on pottery. In the light of present knowledge a better claimant is John Brooks, an Irishman who in 1746 came to Birmingham as an apprentice engraver (6). From there, on 10 September 1751, he applied for a patent in which he claimed:

> '.....the petitioner has by great study application and expense found out a method of printing, impressing and reversing upon enamel and china from engraved, etched and mezzotinto plates, and from cuttings on wood and mettle, impressions of History, Portraits, Landskips, Foliages, Coats of Arms, Cyphers, Letters, Decorations and other Devices. That the said art is entirely new and of his own invention.....'

Brooks moved to Battersea in 1753 to manage the enamel factory and from there made two further applications, 25 January 1754 and April 1755. None of these petitions was successful. In the second application the suitable materials were extended to include stone - and earthenware, and the third added delftware. Birmingham was also a thriving artistic centre as well as being the 'great toyshop of Europe', so that there was no shortage of engravers;

and it was the home of the great printer John Baskerville. It seems clear that it was here that the technique for printing on vitreous surfaces was developed and that it then spread to London, Worcester and Liverpool. The advertisement by Lawrenson (p.6) specifically mentions Birmingham as a centre for the art. Another intriguing figure is Henry Delamain, also an Irishman, who in his application to the Irish Parliament for a patent in 1753 claims that he had 'purchased the art of printing earthenware with as much beauty, strong impression and despatch as can be done on paper'. If he speaks the truth then presumably he purchased the art from Brooks, hoping to apply it to his successful delftware manufactory in Dublin; but in fact no piece of printed delftware has been attributed to him. Delamain also had connections with Liverpool, where he is known to have recruited some of his workmen. It is through contacts in the pottery and printing trades that Sadler must have learnt of the processes and seen in them quite new possibilities. (7)

The fact that Brooks' petitions for a patent were not granted and that Sadler and Green did not pursue theirs suggests that the techniques of transfer-printing were too well-known for any kind of monopoly to be granted. Nevertheless in one respect Sadler's claim was correct, namely that no-one else had thought of applying the technique to tiles. For most of the period of its existence the Sadler and Green manufactory was the only one printing delftware tiles (8); it was only in 1773 that their apprentice, Richard Abbey, set up on his own, but his production seems to have been very modest.

---

6. See WATNEY, 1976 for a detailed discussion of the invention and of the part played by John Brooks.
7. Both Mayer and Gregson had far more fanciful explanations of how he hit upon the idea of printing tiles; see RAY, 1973b, p37.
8. Sadler also printed creamware tiles for Wedgwood; see RAY, 1994b.

The technical aspect of printing tiles

When, in his application for a patent, Brooks referred to 'printing on ceramic surfaces' he meant of course the art of **transferring** printed designs. In the eighteenth century three methods for doing this were evolved. The first process is one described, somewhat vaguely, in two early documents. On 16 May 1766, during a visit to Birmingham, Lady Shelburne visited John Taylor's enamel workshop where, as she recorded in her diary,

> '....he made and enamelled a landscape on top of a box before us which he afterwards gave me as a curiosity for my having seen it done. The method of doing it is this; a stamping instrument managed only by one woman first impressed the picture on paper, which paper is laid even on a piece of white enamel and rubbed hard with a knife or instrument like it, till it is marked upon the box. Then there is spread over it with a brush some metallic colour reduced to a fine powder which adheres to the moist part and, by putting it afterwards into an oven for a few minutes the whole is completed by fixing the colour'.

A similar process was evidently in use in Chelsea in 1755, as recorded by Jean Rouquet, a Frenchman whose book *L'État des Arts en Angleterre* was published in that year. On a visit he speaks of wares 'painted *en camaieu* using a sort of printing process'. It is of considerable interest that Lawrenson's advertisement of 11 February 1757 speaks of 'Prints upon Porcelain, Enamel and Earthern Wares, as lately practised at Chelsea, Birmingham & c.'

When, in 1798, the Liverpool *Student* appealed for information regarding contemporary methods of transfer-printing, a reply came from an engraver, James Poulton, which was published in the following year. Here the process described is glue-bat printing (10). The transfer-medium was formed by pouring into flat pans warm, liquid, gelatinous animal-glue which, on cooling, became firm but flexible, resilient sheets of jelly with some elasticity and about 3mm thick. To print, the copperplate was charged with a fine oil and cleaned off so that the oil was retained only in the engraving. A section of the glue jelly, cut to the size of the engraving to form the transfer bat, was pressed onto the prepared copperplate. The flat, shiny surface of the bat picked up the minute quantities of oil from the engraving and this in turn was transferred by pressing the oily side of the bat onto the surface of the glazed ware. Colouring, in a fine powder form, was then dusted or pounced, as described in Sadler's note-book, over the oily impression. The surplus colour was cleaned off and the piece was fired in the muffle kiln. At the end of the day the glue bats were melted down, and the process started again (11).

For the third process, a printing-press was required. The design was printed from a heated copperplate, using a specially prepared ceramic ink, also heated to prevent adhesion to the copper. A special kind of tissue paper was used soaked in a solution of soapy water, to reduce the absorption of oil in the pigment and ultimately to aid in separating the paper from the transferred image (12). The transfer was laid face down on the specially prepared ceramic surface and rubbed with a flannel wad or wooden spatula to avoid wrinkling and ensure a perfect transfer of the image. Once the paper had been removed, either by wetting or by soaking in a vat, the object could be dried and fired in a muffle kiln at 800-900°. This process is clearly shown in a work of 1827, *A Representation of Manufacturing of Earthenware* (13).

Unfortunately none of the petitions for patents contains any details of the method involved, but it is likely that the processes described above are in a correct historical sequence, and that by c.1770 the second and third were those in general use. The essential difference between them is that with the glue-bat method the printing is done with what may be described as a sticky coloured varnish, the final colour being pounced on afterwards together with a fluxing medium, whereas with the hot-press method the colour is carried by the paper. On the face of it the hot-press method would seem to be quicker, since the press could print so many images at once.

Until recently it was assumed that Sadler produced his tiles using the third method, but this assumption must now be challenged. Many of the earliest tiles were printed from woodblocks, and it would have been quite impossible to use the hot process to transfer the image. At this early date he could well have used the first process described above, but in the 1760s there is good evidence that he used glue-bats. A short entry in the Notebook, of the 1760s to judge by the handwriting, reads 'Then mix it

9. See WATNEY, 1966; WYMAN, 1980; WILLIAMS-WOOD, 1981; and DRAKARD, 1992. Currently experiments in bat-printing are being carried out by Paul Holdaway and others.
10. WYMAN, 1980, p188f.
11. This description is quoted *verbatim* from the account by Drakard in HORNE, 1989.
12. An original tissue is in the Dyson perrins Museum, Worcester; WILLIAMS-WOOD, 1981 p1.8.
13. WILLIAMS-WOOD, 1981, p1.9. See also the excellent illustrated account of the process by Robert Copeland in *Blue and White Transfer-printed Pottery*, Shire Publications, 1982.

with Linseed Oil Varnish and print with it the Glue Way (not from paper) and pounce it' (14). The first group of tiles derived from copperplates (*B* in the Catalogue) often show the minute imperfections and distortions which are characteristic of bat-printing, and there is now a strong body of opinion which believes that these tiles were printed in this way. However, we also know that Sadler used paper transfers, since an entry in the Notebook says as much. At one point he speaks of a specially prepared paper:

> 'Tried it on March 23 with the Paper done on both sides, and pretty thick and they were the finest Impressions I ever saw. As soon as they were put upon the ware I put the saucers into Water, and the Paper left as fine as Could possibly be - quite clean - and the Plate clean'd quite well up.'

Unfortunately, we do not know the year of the entry, but it is certainly possible that in the later stages he used paper transfers for tiles, and that this process was the one adopted by Green (15). Many later tiles have tear-marks and other blemishes more typical of paper-transfers.

The prime requisite in the printing of tiles was a perfectly flat, smooth surface, and it was fortunate that the Liverpool delftware potters of the time were able to manufacture tiles that were ideal for Sadler's purpose. He was friendly with many of the delftware potters, and the blanks must have come from various sources, those of the earlier period being rather thicker than those made later.

Printing on ceramic surfaces has for so long been a straightforward matter that it is easy to forget the difficulties faced by Sadler and others when the art was in its infancy and there were so many problems to be overcome. The first was to make a ceramic ink which would be fine enough to reproduce the lines of the original and yet be resistant to the heat of the kiln. The second was to ensure that the image fused properly with the glaze, and this required a fluxing agent which differed for each variety of body, whether delftware, creamware, saltglaze, porcelain or enamels. The third was to produce a pounce which would enhance the colour and give impact to the image, as well as tonal depth, something which Sadler talks about frequently in his correspondence with Wedgwood. The solution to these problems necessitated much experimentation, and the importance of Sadler's notebooks lies above all in the recipes which he carefully noted down. In many ways he was remarkably successful, but he could not solve all his difficulties. Above all he would have dearly loved to expand his range of colours beyond black, red and brown, but could not find a truly satisfactory formula for green or blue, as he mentioned in the Notebook (16).

THE FIRST SADLER TILES - 1756 - 1761

The tiles printed from woodblocks or line-engravings

Some surviving tiles printed from woodblocks may well predate the documents, but evidently commercial production did not begin until 1756. Since he was at this stage determined to undersell the Dutch it is not surprising that most of the tiles he made were in a sense printed imitations of Dutch tiles. These, like the painted versions, would provide a series of designs in a fireplace, linked by the borders and corners. The fact that they were mostly painted in blue, purple, or brown monochrome also emphasises his intention. It is the 'Louis XV' border (*A1*) above all which makes sense of what may seem to be a piece of exaggeration in the *Affidavit*, where Sadler claims that, whereas a tile-painter could decorate only two tiles in an hour, he himself could print a hundred. Decoration was obviously the most important process in the manufacture of delftware, but it was also the slowest, and the complexity of the 'Louis XV' border and other borders of similar type is such that it could well have taken half an hour to decorate one tile (17). Sadler saw, as Wedgwood was to see soon after, that it was above all by speeding up this process that he would gain the advantage, not to mention that the firing of the decoration took only fifty minutes in a muffle-kiln rather than two days in the normal kiln.

---

14. WYMAN, 1980, p. 195.
15. An examination of a typical Theatrical tile showed that there was a perceptible ridge around the edge of the tile, and that the border extended over the ridge and down to the edge. This strongly suggests the use of a paper transfer.
16. As mentioned below, many of the first tiles were printed in a fine royal blue, and it is hard to explain why he later found the colour so difficult.
17. Ir. P-J Tichelaar, formerly director of the Makkum Pottery, does not believe the figure to be exaggerated.

Many of these early tiles seem to have been printed from wood-blocks, while others may well have been printed from line-engravings; in both cases there is a lack of variety in tone, and the outlines are heavy. It is not known where the wood-blocks were cut, but Price saw a resemblance between the *chinoiserie* design (*A4-2*) and a wood-cut in the *Liverpool Advertiser*, which might suggest that they were done locally. If so, one must acknowledge that the engraver of the rococo designs after Nilson (*A1*, and see Fig.15) was a master of his craft, for these designs, in spite of the medium, manage to convey a true rococo vitality. Other designs, however, seem far more prosaic. The majority of the early tiles have Dutch borders, but some do not have any border and were probably set in a single strip around a fire-place. If most surviving specimens are in monochrome, the coloured specimens of the 'Shepherd Lovers' (*A2-3*) show that Sadler was experimenting with polychrome, doubtless to answer the challenge of the painted tiles.

Looking at the 'woodblock' tiles to-day many would agree that their effect is rather clumsy and mechanical, that the colours are dull and that they lack the impact of the painted tiles which gain so much from their simplicity and directness. Price believed that they were not popular in England at the time and so were exported to the Thirteen Colonies - hence the notable fireplace in the Longfellow House, Cambridge (Mass.) (18) - and this is very likely so. A lack of public response might account for the fact that he began a new and time-consuming venture in May 1757, the *Liverpool Chronicle and Marine Gazette*, which may after all have seemed more profitable to him than the printing of tiles.

The first tiles printed from copper plates

On 11 November 1757 Sadler inserted the following announcement in the *Liverpool Chronicle* : "Mr Sadler being engaged in the Enamelling of Tiles etc. has declined the Printing of this paper in favour of Mr Owen by whom it will be done for the future. But he will continue the Printing Business in all the Branches as heretofore (excepting the News Print) and hopes to have continuance of favour from his friends."

Beside it must be set various other advertisements which appeared in the Liverpool papers at about this time. On 11 February 1757 the *Liverpool Advertiser* carried an announcement offering a half-crown pamphlet which gave details of "the new and curious art of printing or rather re-printing from copper-plate, Prints upon Porcelain, Enamel and Earthen wares, as lately practised at Chelsea, Birmingham etc ...With a true preparation of suitable Colours; and necessary rules of Baking... being the result of innumerable experiments in every branch they tend to. By Thomas Lawrenson, Engraver."

In the *Liverpool Chronicle* for 3 June 1757 there was the following advertisement : "J Evans, engraver, from London, at his house in Williamson's Field, Liverpool, executes Copper Plates, Seals and other engravings in the most elegant manner, and teaches Young Gentlemen etc. to draw on moderate terms etc etc......."

On 9 July 1756, Darley and Edwards' drawing book was advertised, and on 13 December 1758, Robert Sayer's *Complete Drawing Book*.

From these advertisements it is clear that in a short space of time there arrived in Liverpool not only books of designs which were fashionable, but also men skilled in the art of transfer-printing from copper plates onto porcelain and enamels, and engravers capable of supplying suitable designs for such work. Sadler no doubt saw that he could widen his activities to include the printing of porcelain and enamels, and give his tiles the elegance of porcelain decoration. He lost no time in commissioning Evans to engrave designs for use on porcelain and enamels, some of which also appear on tiles, and it is very probable that Evans continued in his employment as supervisor of the engraving department. However, Sadler also made use of the other engravers, both in London and Liverpool. In a letter of 1763 he specifically mentions Samuel Wale as being 'the principal person that designs for us' and calls him a 'Good natur'd Man, and of great Merit'. The reference is to landscape engravings for use on creamware, but presumably he could also have executed tile designs before this date. Another possibility is Henry Roberts, engraver and publisher, whose headpieces for *Clio and Euterpe*, a collection of songs published in 1758-9, not only were used as tile designs (19) but also show the same doll-like heads which can be seen on a number of early Sadler tiles. In Liverpool Sadler may have called on the services of Thomas Lawrenson and Thomas Billinge.

The most notable thing about these early designs engraved between 1758 and perhaps 1761 is that each one has its own border, and it is reasonable to call the tiles with the very elaborate rococo borders, early; those with the simpler scroll borders, rather later. The evidence for

18. PRICE, 1948, pls 2, 3.
19. *C2-1, C3-5.*

such dating is twofold; firstly two designs with the elaborate border (*B3-1* and *B3-4*) are also found on the earliest tiles, and secondly a number of these designs are found printed rather heavily on a greenish-glazed tile noticeably thicker than the average printed tile of the later periods, but corresponding with the body of the earliest tiles. Such tiles have a very experimental look about them.

Another notable feature is Sadler's signature which is found on a number of these designs, either 'Sadler' or 'J. Sadler', by itself or accompanied by the word 'Liverpool' or, in abbreviated form, 'Liverp¹': presumably it was intended as a kind of 'factory mark'. However, only some of the early designs are known with signatures, and we can only guess at the reason for this. The simplest explanation would be that signed examples of the others have not survived, but there are other possibilities; Sadler might have felt he had no need to advertise, since he had a monopoly of the idea, or he might have felt that the signatures detracted from the appearance of the tiles, especially when seen *en masse*. It is certainly reasonable to assume that the signed tiles were printed before the Sadler and Green partnership of 1761, which would have made the signature inappropriate. At this point the signatures could have been erased from the plate, but if, as seems likely, the tiles were bat-printed, it would have been an easy matter to wipe the signature from the printed image. Sometimes the signature is only half-erased, while on others it remains because it is too deeply embedded in the design (20).

The designs on the early Sadler tiles (Group B) fall into various categories, such as French rococo subjects, street-scenes in the manner of Hogarth and Hayman, *chi-noiseries*, scenes from genteel and low life, and so on. The origin of some of these designs is well known, and we can identify the likely sources of others, although it must be stressed that publishers of designs seem to have borrowed from each other very freely. Occasionally the engravers copied a print, such as 'Le May' after the Watteau subject in the *Recueil Julienne* (*B3-10*), or the skating-scene from Lancret's 'Winter' (*B3-12*). *The Ladies' Amusement* provided other designs such as the youths fishing (*B4-7*), the two flower-basket designs (*B2-1, B2-2*), 'Miss Nancy Dawson' (*B4-3*) (Fig.3) and the 'Pine-apple plant' (*B4-12*). In his paper to the English Ceramic Circle in 1946 on the 'Origin of some Ceramic Designs,' Toppin showed two designs from the drawing-book published by John Bowles in 1756-7; and although neither of the designs illustrated in the *Transactions* (21) is found on tiles, the 'Tea Party with a Negro Page' is very reminiscent of one tile-design (*B4-14*), and the next design in the row, only part of which can be seen in Toppin's illustration, is the origin of the Harlequin design found on later tiles (*C4-2, D2-3*) (Fig.1), which shows that this particular drawing-book provided designs over a long period of time. Another leaf in the collection of Mr Norman Stretton has the design of a 'Boy watching a Girl blowing Bubbles' (*B4-8*, Fig.9), while two sheets formerly in the collection of Mr Eric Benton have the designs for the 'Tea-Party with a Maid pouring from a Kettle' (*B4-15*) and the 'Woman churning Butter' (*B6-14*). This last design is also found on painted tiles, either in blue or manganese monochrome, which could well be contemporary with the printed versions (22).

Two designs of this period call for special mention. The

Fig.1

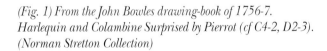

(Fig. 1) From the John Bowles drawing-book of 1756-7.
Harlequin and Colambine Surprised by Pierrot (cf C4-2, D2-3).
(Norman Stretton Collection)

---

20. e.g. *B3-7*
21. *Trans. ECC*, No.10, Vol.2, pl.XCVll.
22. RAY, 1973a, No.210: HORNE, 1989, No.198. We know that the Bowles drawing-book was used by the Liverpool decorators in 1758, since the well-known design of the couple out walking occurs on a Liverpool plate, formerly in the Hemming Collection, with an inscription in Dutch and the date 1758: GARNER, 1972, pl.106B. The design also occurs on painted tiles (RAY, 1973a, No.219 and fig.43), together with a number of other designs.from the same source. See also *C2-3* and *D5-13*.

first is the 'Shepherd and Shepherdess with long Crooks' (*B3-7*), which is one of the very few designs known with different borders. There is little doubt that the rare tile in faded lilac in the Birmingham City Art Gallery is the earlier printing with an experimental border which was rejected in favour of the simpler border seen on the more usual specimens. The other interesting tile-design is that showing a girl dancing before two admirers (*B4-3*), which, although it appears in the *Ladies' Amusement* (Fig.3) without a title, is derived from a print entitled 'Miss Nancy Dawson dancing the Hornpipe'. This is a tile which is found with Sadler's signature and therefore must be an early design; yet it has what is virtually the *88* border. The suggestion is that it was this border, out of the many produced in the early period, which became the standard border when Sadler and Green began producing new designs in the period 1765-70.

One aspect of these and other printed tiles which has never been mentioned in the literature is that a number of designs occur in various 'states' corresponding with the states of an engraving. The obvious reason for this is that the copper-plate gradually became worn through constant use so that the outlines needed strengthening with an engraving tool (23) (Fig.2a & b). Nor is it surprising that the designs which show the greatest variety of detail are precisely those of the period under discussion. The chief differences are to be observed in the sky and in the depth of the engraving, the first printings of some designs being very light and with a carefully lined sky, the later ones being more heavily printed and with a more open sky, often with cross-hatched clouds. Many designs show variations of this kind, and the 'See-saw' (*B6-4*) is one which seems to have been retouched more than most.

As far as the colours are concerned these early tiles are mostly found in black, brown or various shades of iron-red or vermilion, but some are printed in a very pale lilac, which was obviously a difficult colour to control and one which must have been completely lacking in effect. One version of the 'Shepherd and Shepherdess with long Crooks' (*B3-7*), in the Preston Museum, is printed in a turquoise-green which is certainly a deliberate colour and not a misfired black. Indeed it is not always easy to distinguish intentional and unintentional tones of green, and it may well be an error to say that all greens are simply misfired blacks, as Price suggests.

Fig.2a   Fig.2b

(Fig. 2a & b) The print on tile A is sharp and finely detailed. On the later tile B, the engraving has been reworked: note the heavy lines on the girl's skirt, on the table-cloth and under the chair, also the stippling on the faces and the extra clouds added to replace those that had worn away.

(Fig.3) This from plate 32 of the Ladies' Amusement is untitled but it is derived from a print entitled 'Miss Nancy Dawson dancing the Hornpipe'

Fig.3

23. It is also possible that some of these designs were re-engraved.

THE SADLER AND GREEN PERIOD 1761-1770

There is no difficulty in accepting Price's suggestion that it was when Sadler undertook to print Wedgwood's creamware that he took Guy Green into partnership, the earliest known document on which their names appear together being a Wedgwood invoice of September 1761. No doubt Sadler foresaw a greater volume of work than he could cope with alone, and in any case he needed help to carry out further experiments, since the creamware glaze and body differ so much from delftware. It took them some months to perfect the technique of printing on creamware, but, having done so, they found themselves overwhelmed with orders from Wedgwood and, as can be seen from the Sadler letters quoted by Price, they had relatively little time for printing tiles, even though these were in great demand. Moreover the copper-plates for creamware had to be specially engraved (24).

Presumably, therefore, at this date they continued to print tiles whenever possible from the old plates, reworking them where necessary and erasing any signatures in deference to Green, and had little time to commission and print new tile designs. However, the first group of ship tiles, with rococo scroll borders, might date from 1761-3, the evidence for this being that one of the tiles in the group (B9-2) bears the signature 'Sadler Liverpool' while one example of the second (B9-4) has the unique signature 'Sadler C Liverpool' which, it is suggested, stands for Sadler and Company, in recognition of the new partnership (25).

It is only in August 1764 that we find in a letter from Sadler to Wedgwood the sentence, 'We have been very busy at tiles and have done 60 patterns towards 100'. The meaning is not very clear, but it may indicate that at about this time they began to think of expanding their range of designs. Perhaps it was at this moment also that the 88 border became the standard border for all the new designs, mainly, one imagines, because it provided the type of repeating framework which is a feature of the painted tiles and which gave unity to the fireplace in spite of the diversity of designs. This was something that the earlier tiles would have done less well. Why exactly the border of 'Miss Nancy Dawson' (B4-3) was chosen is not clear, but it may have been because it was the only one to have the figure-of-eight motif, which punctuates the vertical border in a dominant manner. It is impossible to say which designs with the 88 border were commissioned before Sadler's retirement in 1770, but it is reasonable to suppose that the two designs which show earlier designs in reverse - 'Ruins with a Bridge' (D7-1) and the 'Lady and Gentleman with a Pine-apple Plant (D4-11)- were among the first together with those also found on the polychrome tiles (C2-C5).

By 1767 Sadler could advertise 'upwards of 100 designs' of 'Landskips, Ruins, Ships, Pictures, Rural figures etc', the kind of tiles illustrated in section D, which all have the 88 border.

The tiles with the 88 border are mostly found printed in black or red, but specimens printed in sepia are not uncommon. Other colours proved more difficult. Just before he retired in 1770 Sadler wrote in the Notebook, 'made several essays towards a purple colour some time ago but find it very difficult. We shall not give up'; from this one might infer that the version of the 'Drunken Peasant singing' (D5-14), which is printed in a strong purple, was printed after 1770, at the same time as the four Fable tiles in the Liverpool Museum mentioned below. The purple would have been an expensive as well as a tricky colour, since gold was an essential ingredient. Blue also caused much difficulty. In the 1760s Worcester developed the art of printing in underglaze-blue, and this may have inspired Sadler to try his hand at producing tiles printed in blue. Such tiles were mentioned in the 1767 advertisement, and an entry in the Notebook dated 20 July 1768, records the making of a glaze for creamware which was 'vastly good also as good as can be for blue tiles'. Yet he failed to hit upon a satisfactory recipe for a blue ceramic ink. In September 1769 he wrote, 'every now and then we are trying at a Blue and Green colour that wd (sic) be good & print as well as Old Black'. When one considers that so many of the tiles from the earliest period were printed in a striking royal blue it is surprising that the colour later proved so difficult (26).

The sources of the later designs are on the whole better known. Once more the John Bowles drawing-book provided a number of subjects; not only the Harlequin design already mentioned (Fig.1) but also the 'Peasant with a Wine-bottle and Glass' (D5-13) (Fig.14b), the 'Peasant Family with a Cradle' (D5-10) (Fig.14a) and the 'Couple on a Bench and a Child with a Doll' (D4-5) (Fig. 13). The Ladies Amusement provided the scenes of the 'Sailor offering a Present to a Girl' (D5-8) and the 'Young Man doffing his Hat to two Ladies' (D4-1) and this last is one of the few designs known which also appeared on the painted tiles, as a fragment in the Liverpool Museum shows.

Two groups of tiles call for special mention - those with the printed design enamelled in polychrome (C2-C5) and the borderless ship tiles (C1).

---

24. STRETTON (1970) discusses the seventeen subjects mentioned by Sadler in a letter to Wedgwood written in March 1763. Some of these designs also occur on tiles, but from different plates: e.g.'Harvest Home' (C3-5), 'The Tea Party' (B6-1), 'Harlequin and Columbine' (D2-3) and the 'Society of Bucks' (B1-2).
25. The first tile in the group (B9-1) appears to be one of the earliest designs done from copper-plates.
26. For the only known late tile printed in blue (D4-15a) see below.

Sadler had already experimented with enamel colours, as is shown by *A2-3*, and it seems that he took up the idea again in about 1766. An entry in the notebook for January 1767 gives the recipes for 'Enamel colours for China and Tiles', including a yellow, dark and light green, orange, rose and blue (27). Production of such polychrome tiles must have begun soon after, since the following advertisement appeared in the *Liverpool General Advertiser* for 1 May 1767:

PRINTED WARE MANUFACTORY in Harrington Street continue to sell wholesale and retail at very moderate prices Printed, enamelled and japanned CHINA, Also CREAM-COLOURED ware and TILES &c,viz. complete services of cream colour as Terrines, Dishes and Plates of all sizes; bowls, decanters, mugs, coffee pots, teapots and every other article.
Fine Copper Plate Printed and enamelled TILES of different colours, viz.Black, Red, Chocolate, Blue and White and coloured after nature.
*   N.B. Cream coloured ware is the best and most elegant. Ships and Patterns made and engraved and ornamented with a very great variety of masterly subjects properly adapted to each piece of ware; and the TILES are neater than any done in Holland, or elsewhere, consisting of upwards of a hundred different patterns of Landskips, Ruins, Ships, Pictures, Rural figures & c. The engraving for which has cost upwards of £800 and the printing is as good as it is possible to have done.*

This shows that the tiles 'coloured after nature' were then a stock item. On some of these tiles the colour is thinly applied, allowing much of the detail of the engraving to show through; on others the enamelling is thick and coarse. It may well be that Sadler, again with an eye to rivalling the painted tiles, was inspired by the hand-coloured plates in the *Ladies Amusement* and other drawing-books.

These tiles were among those exported to New England, and it is there that the finest specimens are still to be seen in their original setting. Price and others mention the damaged fireplace with such tiles in the Lee Mansion, Marblehead (Virginia), a house built for Colonel Jeremiah Lee between 1767 and 1769 (28). Other places where these rare tiles are to be found include Rhode Island House, Newport (R.I.) (29), and the Fayerweather House, Cambridge (Mass.), apparently built in the mid-1760s (30), while the Bostonian Society has two tiles which came from the parlour of the Phillips House in Cross Street, Boston (31). In England there are isolated tiles in the British Museum, in the Sheffield Museum and in private collections.

Some of the designs are only found on these polychrome tiles, but others are variants of designs better known in monochrome. The word 'variants' is important, since a striking thing about these tiles, apart from the colouring, is that nearly all of them were printed from specially engraved plates without a border. Price states 'in this instance it is interesting that the scrolled border was removed from the print', but in fact only three of the designs appear to be from the same plates as the monochrome versions - the 'Tea-party' (*C2-6*), 'The Blind Man carrying the Lame' (*C4-1*) and 'The Fortune-teller' (*C3-6*). Some designs look back to the earlier tiles - e.g. The 'Peasant with Barrel and Girl with a Rake' (*C3-4*), 'The Sailor's Farewell' (*C3-7*), 'Shuttlecock and Battledore' (*C2-2*) and 'Rustic Lovers interrupted by an Old Woman' (*C3-9*) - while others correspond with designs with the *88* border; e.g. 'The Nursemaid' (*C2-4*), 'Shepherd and Shepherdess' (*C3-2*), 'The Fortune-teller' (*C3-6*), 'The Blind Man carrying the Lame' (from a print published about 1764-5), 'Harlequin and Columbine' (*C4-2*), 'The Turkish Merchant' (*C5-2*) and the 'Chinese figures with a Chime of Bells' (*C5-1*).

The sources of some of the designs, hitherto unpublished, are those already mentioned - the 'Harvest Home' (*C3-5*) and the 'Gallant and Lady by a Stile' (*C2-1*) are probably from head-pieces in Clio and Euterpe, Vol 1 (1758), while the 'Fortune-teller' (*C3-6*) (Fig.11) and the 'Gallant playing the Flute to a Lady' (*C2-3*) (Fig.10) are found side by side in the John Bowles drawing-book, the latter design also occurring on a Liverpool painted tile in the Bristol City Art Gallery. More curiously the design of the 'Shepherd and Shepherdess' (*C3-1*) occurs on a late Liverpool jug in the Liverpool Museum, with an inscription 'A Present from Liverpool', albeit from a different engraving.

The rarity of these tiles seems to indicate that they were no more successful than the coloured 'woodblock' tiles, and they may have been exported for the same reason. It cannot be said that the colouring is very effective.

---

27. For these recipes see PRICE (1948) p.91.
28. PRICE, 1948, p.51; and see also BRIDGES, 1978, pp.174-183. The fireplace has *C2-1* (two), *C2-3* (two), *C2-5* (three), *C3-1* (two), *C3-6* and *C3-7* (two). An article on the house, by Helen Hall, was published in Country Life, 30 January 1972.
29. BRIDGES, 1978, pls 92,93. The designs illustrated are *C1-6, C2-1, C2-2, C2-3, C3-9, C4-2* (two) and *C5-1* (two).
30. RAY, 1973b, p44. The tiles in the parlour include *C2-1* (two), *C2-3* (three), *C2-4, C2-5* (two), *C3-1* (three), *C3-3* (two), *C3-4* (two), *C3-5* (two) and *C5-1*.
31. RAY, 1973a, Nos.673 (*C3-3*) and 674 (*C3-7*).

The ship-tiles in the second group are very different from the first. Apart from the fact that they do not have a border and are printed in a pale grey, they seem to aim for authenticity in the portrayal of the vessels rather than the creation of a dramatic effect; the juxtaposition, in the Liverpool Museum, of one of these tiles showing a pilot cutter (*C1-1*) and a model of a similar craft is very telling. The designs appear to be taken directly from marine prints, or perhaps a book illustrating ship-types (32). In view of the fact that the other group of borderless tiles is mentioned in the 1767 advertisement, it is possible that these are the 'Ships' which he was also offering.

Some printing was done on delftware, probably between 1760 and 1765, but very few pieces have survived. The second version of the 'Sailors Farewell' (*B6-22*), found on two plates (33), is from the same engraving as the tile design, as is the 'Sportsman's Arms' (*B1-1*) (cf.Fig.7). A bowl in the Victoria and Albert Museum has in the centre the King of Prussia, evidently from the engraving commissioned by Sadler for use on porcelain in 1758 and signed 'Sadler Liverp[l] Enl Evans Sc', but the fact that the other print is of General Wolfe taken from an engraving of 1763, also for use on porcelain, shows that the bowl must have been printed in 1763-4. 'The Tythe-pig', found on two mugs (cf.Fig.4) and two plates, is in reverse to the tile design (*B6-1*) and differs in the detail. It is signed 'J.Sadler Liverpool', which either suggests a date before 1761 or else confirms that the partnership with Green only applied to the printing of tiles and creamware, leaving Sadler free to print on porcelain or delftware(34).

(Fig.4) 'The Tythe Pig' (cf B6-1) A transfer-printed, tin-glazed mug .

THE GREEN PERIOD 1770 - ?1790

Shortly after the death of his father in October 1765 John Sadler decided to give up press printing; an entry in the Notebook, dated 1 January 1766, reads, 'Messrs Everard and Co took all the printing utensils out of my office'. What is precisely meant by the word 'all' is uncertain. If it is taken in the literal sense it would imply that from then on no printed paper-transfers were used, whereas we know from other entries that he was extremely pleased with the results obtained by such transfers. Perhaps on account of ill-health it seems that Sadler was becoming weary of running the business, for at about this time in 1766-7 he thought of taking on another partner, giving as his reason 'J.Sadler's not chusing to confine himself to business as here tofore'. This is the explana-

tion given in what is in fact the first entry of the Notebook as bound today, and it accompanies a draft of the conditions for such a partnership. Either the matter was not pursued or else no-one was prepared to buy himself into the enterprise on the stiff terms offered. However, it was in 1767 that Richard Abbey was taken on as an apprentice. Sadler retired in 1770, leaving Green to carry on the manufactory, but he did not lose interest in the technical aspects of tile printing. The experiments continued, presumably at Harrington Street, and the results recorded in the Notebook were doubtless passed on to Green. As mentioned above, it is uncertain for how long Green continued to print tiles; the year 1790 is conjectural.

Presumably Green at first continued to make use of

32. WATNEY (1993), discusses William Jackson of Liverpool, a ship painter whose work seems to have inspired the pottery and porcelain decorators. He specifically mentions *B9-8* as being in the 'Jackson style'. He also mentions the strange fact that contemporary marine prints hardly exist today.
33. GARNER 1972, pl.115B
34. cf SMITH, 1970, pl.4.

the large stock of copper-plates which had been built up in the 1760s, especially those with the *88* border, but he soon commissioned other designs in this style, as is shown by the dates of the engravings used; 'The Pluralist and the Old Soldier' (*D3-1*) and 'A Six Weeks Tour to Paris' (*D3-4*) are both of 1770, while the engravings by Grignion after Brandoin (*D3-5, D3-6, D3-25, D3-26,* and *D3-27*) are of 1771-2 and the chinoiserie tile (*D6-3*) is from a Pillement engraving of 1774. The latter sometimes has the signature 'Green', and a possible explanation for this is that Green wanted to differentiate his tiles from those of Abbey, who had set up on his own in the previous year. One late design (*D2-8*) was called by Watson 'An Allegory of the French Revolution', but this identification must be wrong, since it is improbable that any designs were com-missioned as late as 1789. The scene appears rather to depict Don Quixote being cured of his madness by an allegorical figure of Wisdom (35). Another interesting tile is *D4-15a* which has the shooting party after Stubbs but in reverse, with an individual border and printed in blue. The date of the engraving is 1769, and so this could well be an early experiment by Green to see if he could print in this difficult colour. The fact that it is the only known late tile in blue may indicate that he was unable to find a satisfactory recipe. All these tiles carry on the earlier tradition, but three series of tiles represent a new departure - those illustrating Aesop's Fables, which Green, according to Price, certified as being his commission after Sadler's retirement (36); the Neo-classical tiles; and the Theatrical tiles.

Fable Tiles

Fable subjects became very popular on English ceramics in the third quarter of the 18th century. The vogue apparently started with Chelsea 'red anchor' and Worcester porcelain with designs by O'Neale and others, and similar subjects are found on salt-glaze (37). Two fable subjects on printed tiles evidently date from c. 1765-70 (*D3-7*) showing the fable of 'The Fable of the Sticks', and (*D3-8*) showing 'The Blind carrying the Lame' - neither of them from *Aesop*, and both in the style of the other tiles in group D.

Inspiration for the Aesop designs came from two main sources (38) - Francis Barlow (1626-1704), whose great folio Aesop was published by Thomas Rycroft in 1665, and Sébastien Le Clerc (1633-1714). Their interpretations of the fables established a canon which others were happy to copy. One such imitator was Elisha Kirkall (1682-1742) who engraved the plates for Samuel Croxall's *Fables of Aesop and Others*, taking eighty-three designs from Barlow, twenty-seven from Le Clerc and fifteen from Francois Chauveau's engravings for La Fontaine's *Fables* (1668).Croxall's work was first published in 1722 and by the middle of the century it had already run to five editions. It is also interesting to note that on 17 December 1759 a pack of playing-cards was advertised by I.Kirk of the Grotto Toy Shop, St. Paul's Churchyard - 'Aesop's Fables exactly copied after Barlow, with Fables and Morals in verse' (39). Such a pack could have easily suggested to Green the idea of a set of tiles, but, though the style of engraving is very similar, only thirteen of the subjects appear in the same form on both playing-cards and tiles. The forty-five designs on the tiles all derive from Croxall, but the finely engraved plates are infinitely superior to Kirkall's simple line-engravings.

All the tiles in the Fable series have the *88* border, and one, 'The Fowler and Ringdove'(*D8-17*), also has a square frame inside the border. The great majority of surviving tiles are printed in black, either on a white or, more rarely, a pale blue ground, but they also are found printed in brown and in purple, four tiles in the Liverpool Museum being in this last colour. Even more extraordinary is the turquoise-green version of the 'Lark and her Young Ones' (*D8-31*) in the Preston Museum (40).

Of particular interest are the Wedgwood creamware plates printed with Fable designs in reddish brown from the same copper-plates as those used for the tiles. Fifteen such plates have survived, and they make an interesting contrast with the saltglaze plates with fable subjects taken directly from Barlow, printed in red but with the rim enamelled in turqoise-blue (41).

35. WATSON , 1927. The episode is illustrated in a similar fashion in a French edition of *Don Quixote* published in 1742. The engraving, by J. von Schley after Coypel, is entitled 'Don Quichotte est délivré de sa folie par la Sagesse'.
36. PRICE, 1948, p.94b (addenda sheet); he does not give his source.
37. For example the moulded tiles from Whieldon's house with designs from John Gay's Fables (RAY, 1994b, p.195f). See also STRETTON, 1994, p.205f.
38. For a review of these sources see WATNEY, 1987.
39. There is a complete pack in the Cincinnati Art Museum, John Omwake Collection; six examples are illustrated in Catherine Perry's *History of Playing Cards*, p.203.
40. The difficulties experienced in printing in purple and green are mentioned above.
41. The Wedgwood plates are in the Schreiber Collection (Cat. Vol.11 No. 401 a-l) and the British Museum. The salt-glaze examples are discussed by STRETTON (1994).

Neo-Classical Tiles

It is convenient to group together all the green enamelled designs under the heading of neo-classical tiles, although the term is occasionally a misnomer. Guy Green refers to these tiles in a letter to Wedgwood of 1776, stating that the green-enamelled tiles were 4/6d a dozen, the white-ground variety 4/- a dozen. The tiles were clearly inspired by Wedgwood; indeed one design, 'Hercules between Vice and Virtue' (*E1-1*), not only copies a Wedgwood and Bentley plaque of 1777 but also imitates the Birmingham ormolu mount (Fig. 20). As Watney has shown (42), further designs are taken from an edition of Horace published in 1749, with engravings by J.S. Müller. He mentions three subjects - 'Fortune' (*E1-8*) (Fig.19b), the 'Muse' (*E1-7*), and the 'Three Graces' (*E1-9*). Another source is *Polymetis* by Edward Spence, published by R.Dodsley in 1747, with engravings by Boitard (43); 'Diana' (*E1-3*), 'Mercury' (*E1-4*) and 'Bacchus' (*E1-5*) come from this source and it should be noted that the work also contains variants of 'Fortune', 'The Three Graces' and 'Apollo' which appear in the 'Horace'.

The vase designs reflect the contemporary fashion for antique vases which Wedgwood described as 'vase madness'. As Clifford has shown (44), many collections of such vases were published, both in England and abroad, but only one of these can presently be shown to have inspired Guy Green. This is Matthew Darly's collection of 1770 (45), from which nine of the tile-designs have been taken, sometimes with minor alterations. Like the classical subjects, the vases and urns of the E1 group are very finely engraved with elaborate borders which show the same complexity as those of the theatrical tiles.

Green gives the prices of the two styles, either printed with the outlines enamelled in green on a white ground, or with the design printed on a green enamelled ground; but only some of the designs are known today in both versions. Their aim is to imitate antique gems and cameos, and in this they succeed admirably, thanks to the fineness of the engraving. The colour is usually a strong apple-green, but occasionally it takes on a faintly bluish appearance.

Theatrical Tiles

In the final decades of the eighteenth century there was a considerable vogue for theatrical portraits, both painted and engraved, and the tiles are a reflection of this fashion. They form two distinct groups, one with a highly complex border, the other far simpler. The relationship between the two is not clear, but it may well have been Richard Abbey who first portrayed actors and actresses on tiles (see below), and who inspired Green to produce the more elaborate series. Price suggests that London was the chief outlet for these tiles, since the actors and actresses would not be well-known outside the capital, but Parkinson has pointed out that some of them appeared on the stage in Manchester, and indeed some were born locally (46).

The designs for these tiles come from four sources - Robert Sayer's *Dramatic Characters, or Different Portraits of the English Stage*, with engravings variously dated between 1769 and 1772; Bell's *British Theatre and Shakespeare of 1776-7* (47); and Lowndes' *New English Theatre* of 1777. In the first group of Theatrical tiles (*F1*) two designs (*F1-8* and *F1-31*) are from Sayer, but the rest are from Bell and Lowndes, apart from three (*F1-16, F17* and *F1-18*) for which no engraved source has yet been found. The engravings for the tiles seem to be the work of one man and they were presumably done at one time, the earliest possible date for such a commission being 1777. At such a late date they may have been in production for a very limited period.

For these tiles a special border was designed, with flaming torches, masks, musical instruments and weapons suggestive of the theatre; and the detail of the costumes is extremely fine. The majority of the tiles are printed in black, but a number have survived printed in a reddish brown of a tone similar to that on some Fable tiles.

---

42. WATNEY, 1972.
43. 'POLYMETIS or an Enquiry concerning the AGREEMENT Between the works of the ROMAN POETS And REMAINS of the ANTIENT ARTISTS, being an attempt to illustrate them mutually from one another by the Revd. Mr Spence'. Printed for R. Dodsley; at Tully's-Head, Pall Mall, 1747.
44. TIMOTHY CLIFFORD, 'Some English Ceramic Vases and their Sources, Part 1' (*Trans, ECC.* Vol 10, Part 3, 1978).
45. *55 Vases* by M. Darley, 'Published by Mr Darley according to the Act. 31st, August 1770 where may be had Variety of Vases and other Ornaments'; VAM Departments of Prints and Drawings 28097,1-50).
46. MICHAEL PARKINSON 'The Incomparable Art', Catalogue of the Greg Collection, Manchester City Art Gallery, 1969, p.45f. He specifically mentions Mrs Abington, Lee-Lewis and Mrs Ward.
47. Many of the original water-colour drawings for Bell's publications, by Roberts and Parkinson, are in the Burney Collection of Theatrical Portraits in the British Museum.

Pattern Tiles

In the creation of overall patterns the advantages of the printing process counted for far less, and it does not seem as if many such designs were produced. The diaper pattern on *G1-2*, which was evidently commonly found on Liverpool clock-faces, would certainly have produced a drab effect, and the printed flower-head pattern (*G1-1*) is in no way superior to the painted version. An entry in the Notebook for 19 February 1774 reads, 'printing Blue Tiles Marble and Black tiles Marble'. Perhaps this is a loose reference to the diaper pattern, since it would be impossible to create a true marbled effect by any engraved process. Certainly these tiles appear to date from the 1770s.

Border Tiles

Half-size tiles for borders were standard product of the delftware tile-makers (48), and a small number of printed designs have survived. That with the design from *Dodsley's Fables* (*G2-1*) may be the earliest; at all events it is the finest, showing a remarkable delicacy of outline. The other types are later, being made to accompany either the Theatrical or the Neo-Classical tiles; *G2-2* is in fact a reduced version of the border of the main series of Theatrical tiles, with a candelabrum rather than an actor or actress in the centre. The function of *G2-3* is uncertain, since it is enamelled in an unfortunate combination of green and pinkish mauve. It would have ruined the effect of the green enamelled tiles and one can only suggest that it was designed to enclose panels of plain white tiles.

RICHARD ABBEY

Abbey was born in 1754 and apprenticed to Sadler in 1767 as an engraver, Sadler having by then sold his printing machinery. At the end of his apprenticeship, in1773, he set up his own business in Clieveland Square, putting the following advertisement in the *Liverpool Advertiser* for 10 December 1773:

RICHARD ABBEY
Late apprentice to Messrs Sadler and Green begs leave to inform his friends and the public;
That he has open'd his shop at No.11 in Clieveland Square Where he manufactures and sell all sorts of Queen's Ware Printed in the neatest manner and in Variety of Colours.
N.B. Orders of exportation
Also crests, coats of arms, Tiles or any other particular devices will be completed at the shortest notice. By their most obedient, humble servant, Richard Abbey.

In 1777 he evidently gave up his business there and nothing is known of his activities until his reappearance in Toxteth in 1794. He died in 1819.

The wording of the advertisement shows that he printed creamware and that he engraved special designs to order. In Sadler's advertisement of 1767 tiles are listed as part of the stock in trade; here they appear to be rather a bespoke item, and it is unlikely that there was a large production, since he only ran his business in Clieveland Square for four years. A number of pieces of later Liverpool and Staffordshire pottery have prints with his signature, which, as Smith points out (49), confirms that he was principally a free-lance engraver to the pottery trade.

It is uncertain what work he may have done for Green. Unless he was precocious, which is unlikely in the view of the rather coarse effect of his later signed work, he could not possibly have engraved the Fables or the Neo-Classical tiles, and the prints which inspired the first group of theatrical tiles (*F1*) were only published at about the time he left Liverpool (50). The second group of theatrical tiles (*F2*) can certainly be ascribed to him, since one of them (*F2-3*) is signed 'Abbey Liverpool'. This small group of tiles, which now includes six subjects, differs greatly from the first group, producing a far simpler effect. The designs come from Robert Sayer's *Dramatic Characters* (1769-72), where the prints are on the same scale as those on the tiles and are less flamboyant than those in Bell's or Lowndes' publications, while the husk border is very modest compared with that of the first group. They must

48. RAY 1973a, Nos.598-602; HORNE, 1989, Nos.397-402.
49. SMITH, 1970, pp.15-19.
50. A version, on a larger scale of David Garrick as Don John, after Lowndes (cf.*F1-10*), which appears on a Liverpool creamware jug (Liverpool Museum), has been attributed to Abbey.

have been produced in the four years 1773-7, at which date he could only have used Sayer's prints, and it seems very likely that he was in fact the first to print tiles with such subjects, perhaps to special order; their rarity today compared with those of the first group might confirm this suggestion.

The same kind of simplicity of design and border is apparent in the second group of vase tiles (*E3*), and it is very probable that these are also his work. Seven designs are known, compared with the seventeen of the main series, but very few specimens have survived, the most important group being at Sudbury Hall, Derbyshire.

CONCLUSION

Something must be said about the setting of these printed tiles. As far as one can tell, they were only used in fireplaces of modest size, usually in bedrooms or parlours. Unfortunately, as a result of demolition and reconstruction in the nineteenth century, the original installations have nearly all vanished in England, although there are some thirty examples extant in the United States. Since fireplace tiles are particularly liable to damage, it is unlikely that any surviving installation is exactly as it was originally; indeed many of them have obviously been patched up with whatever tiles happened to be available, either printed or painted, as may be seen by looking at the fireplaces in the Longfellow House which even include Dutch painted tiles (51). Few fireplaces in England have survived intact, but at least those at Croft Castle, a building which was being renovated and refurnished in the1760s, seem to be original. Here too tiles have been reset or replaced, but there are a number of signed tiles - in one fireplace seven out of sixteen tiles are signed - and the earlier designs predominate; these may well have formed part of the original installations. Three of the fireplaces also suggest that the tiles were always set symmetrically, with the designs balancing out on each side. This is also a feature of the fireplaces illustrated by Bridges (52), allowing for breakage and replacement, and also in contemporary fireplaces with painted tiles. Such an arrangement would in fact be the only way of avoiding a very jumbled effect. Whether the customer himself chose the designs from some kind of pattern-book (53), or whether the contractor simply supplied what was available, is a matter for speculation.

The dressing-room fireplace at Sudbury Hall, already referred to, is known to have been put together by the estate carpenter in the 1920s, but the actual tiles, whose neo-classical solemnity clashes with the extravagant Jacobean wood-carving of the over-mantel, are doubtless set as they might have been originally. A number of fireplaces in America also have single strips of tiles framing the opening. An arrangement of a different kind is suggested by the panel of neo-classical tiles 'from a house in Reigate' in the Victoria and Albert Museum (54); these must have occupied some kind of wall space, if they are framed as originally installed.

As Lane pointed out in his *Guide to Tiles*, it was an aesthetic mistake to fill a fireplace with a series of designs which, like book-illustrations, must be seen from up close. At a distance the details become blurred, and the bold impact of the painted tiles is entirely lacking. Nor indeed can it be said that the borders play any significant part in the overall effect. Paradoxically, these utilitarian objects, always conceived as elements in an overall decorative scheme, are most easily appreciated as individual objects whose interest lies mainly in the subject-matter which says so much about contemporary taste.

---

51. PRICE , 1948, pls. 2 and 3.
52. BRIDGES, 1978; see especially pls. 88a and b, 91 and 92. If, as is likely, these contain the original tiles, the presence of pairs of designs is in itself significant.
53. Very little is known about the marketing of these tiles, but the idea that there were pattern-books is suggested by the print on ordinary paper of a tile-design with an *88* border (Ray, 1974, pl.105a); It is not known on surviving tiles. Naturally this print could have been taken from the plate later for some other purpose.
54. ARTHUR LANE, *Guide to Tiles*, 1939, pl.40, *E3-1*, the only recorded example, comes from this panel.

A - The First Sadler Tiles 1756 - 7

Fig.5
Rococo designs from the series of prints entitled
'Caffe, The und Tobac Zieretten' by
J. E. Nilson of Augsburg

A1-1

A1-2

A1-3

A1-4

A1-5

A1-6

A1-7

A1-8

A1-9

A1-1　A lady and gentleman in hunting costume by a *rocaille* (Fig.5a).

A1-2　A girl and a man smoking in a rococo arbour (Fig.5b).

A1-3　A girl at a table accompanied by a man smoking.

A1-4　A gallant kissing a girl's hand, with a Cupid perched on a *rocaille* (Fig.5c).

A1-5　A boy with a jug on a table, and a girl with a rake, against a *rocaille.*

A1-6　A girl and a shepherd with a crook in a *rocaille.* In the original design (Fig.5d) the boy holds a long pipe.

A1-7　A turbanned figure sitting astride a *rocaille.*

A1-8　A turbanned figure holding a pipe, and another pouring tea from a fantastic urn (Fig.5e).

A1-9　Two Chinese figures by a leafy *rocaille* (Fig.5f).

A - The First Sadler Tiles 1756 - 7 (continued)

A1-10

A1-11

A1-12

A1-10 A soldier in a feathered hat, with a sword, bowing to a lady seated on the ground; background of fantastic ruins and shrubs.

A1-11 A gentleman in an elaborate tricorne hat smoking a pipe, seated on a *rocaille*, on which a tankard is perched.

A1-12 A turbanned figure smoking a long pipe, a kettle by his side.

A 2 - Other 'European' Subjects

A2-1

A2-2

A2-3

A2-4

A2-5

A2-6

A2-1 A girl sitting on a mound; trees and buildings behind.

A2-2 'The Sailor's Return' outside the 'Lion of Scotland'. See also *B6-21*.

A2-3 Shepherd lovers with a dog. These tiles are either blue monochrome or printed in black and enamelled in colours. cf. *B3-4*.

A2-4 A shepherd walking a sleeping shepherdess. cf. *B3-1*, either blue monochrome or printed in black and enamelled in colours.

A2-5 A village scene with a young man and girl dancing to the music of a man playing a shawm.

A2-6 An elegant couple with haymakers.

A 3 - Literary Sources

A3-1

A3-1　A scene from a novel or a play.

A 4 - Chinoiserie Subjects

A4-1　　　　　　　　　　　　　A4-2　　　　　　　　　　　　　A4-3

A4-1　Two Chinese figures by an altar under a canopy, with attendant. The design is after an unsigned *chinoiserie* print (Fig.6).

A4-2　A Chinaman fishing accompanied by a girl; a pavilion in the background. A variant, with only one tree on the left, is in the Longfellow House, Cambridge (Mass.).

A4-3　?Chinese figures with animals by a river. The 'Dutch' border is derived from Liverpool painted tiles imitating a Dutch type.

A3-2　An unsigned and undated *chinoiserie* print depicting an altar, evidently the source of the 'woodblock' tile, *A4-1* (formerly Eric Benton Collection).

Fig. 6

A 5 - Landscapes and Buildings

A5-1

A5-2

A5-3

A5-4

A5-5

A5-6

A5-7

A5-8

A5-9

A5-1   A terrace and ruined portico.

A5-2   A man with a dog by an inn.

A5-3   A canal scene in Holland.

A5-4   A landscape with a peasant couple accompanied by donkeys, goats and sheep. The design is from 'Le Soir', an engraving by J. P. Le Bas after N. Berchem (Watney, 1987 pl.48).

A5-5   A canal scene with swans; large building to the right, and buildings with turrets to the left.

A5-6   A ruined portico, with a statue and figures.

A5-7   A riverscape with trees and houses, and a man driving a cow.

A5-8   A riverscape with domed building to the right and a bridge; other buildings to the left, and a man fishing in the foreground (for the border of cf.*A4-3*).

A5-9   A tower and ?ruined church by a river, with a man fishing.

A 5 - Landscapes and Buildings (continued)

A5-10

A5-11

A5-12

A5-13

A5-14

A5-15

A5-10 A ruin and buildings by a river, with boatman.
A5-11 Buildings by a river, with a woman and a man fishing.
A5-12 A gazebo with cottage and figures.
A5-13 A ruined temple with two figures, one seated.
A5-14 A ruined temple with two figures, one pointing.
A5-15 Landscape with buildings and a peasant riding a donkey.

A 6 - Marine Subjects

A6-1 A sailing boat in a gale. Probably after Zeeman or Bakhuyzen.

A6-1

B - EARLY SADLER TILES PRINTED FROM COPPER - PLATES WITH INDIVIDUAL BORDERS 1757-1761

B 1 - Armorial Tiles

B1-1

B1-1a

B1-2

(Fig.7) Liverpool tin-glazed plate, printed with the Sportsman's Arms (*B1-1*).

B1-2a

B1-3

B1-1   The Sportsman's Arms. Sometimes found signed *Sadler Liverpool*.
B1-1a   The same design but without the scrolls in the border.
B1-2   The Arms of the Society of Bucks. Sometimes found signed *Sadler Liverpool*.
B1-2a   The same design but with a formal border.
B1-3   Masonic emblems and mottos - 'Amor, Honor et Justitia' and 'Sit Lux et Lux Fuit'.

B 2 - Flower Baskets

B2-1

B2-2

B2-1   A basket of flowers. Sometimes found signed *Sadler Liverp¹*. The design is from the *Ladies Amusement*, Pl.6.
B2-2   An overturned basket with birds. The design taken from the *Ladies Amusement*, Pl.74.

B 3 - French Rococo Subjects

B3-1

B3-2

B3-3

B3-4

B3-5

B3-6

B3-7

B3-7a

B3-8

B3-1   A shepherd walking a sleeping shepherdess. cf. the earlier version, *A2-4*.

B3-2   A gallant offering a girl a bird's nest. Sometimes found signed *J. Sadler Liverp¹*. The design appears to be taken from a plate in the John Bowles drawing-book.

B3-3   A rustic couple with a dog.

B3-4   Shepherd lovers with a dog. Sometimes found signed *J. Sadler Liverp¹*. The design is adapted from Boucher's painting 'Les Amours Pastorales'. cf. the earlier version, *A2-3*.

B3-5   A shepherd piping to a shepherdess. Sometimes found signed *J. Sadler Liverp¹*.

B3-6   Shepherd lovers holding arms beneath a tree. Sometimes found signed *Sadler Liverpool*.

B3-7   A shepherd and shepherdess holding long crooks. Sometimes found signed *Sadler Liverpool*.

B3-7a The same design with a different border.

B3-8   A lady with a guitar, Cupid with a torch. Sometimes found signed *J. Sadler Liverpool*.

B3-9

B3-10

B3-11

B3-9 A man playing a lute and a girl singing.

B3-10 A man dancing to the bagpipes. Sometimes found signed *J. Sadler Liverpool*. The design is adapted from Watteau's 'Le May', engraved by Aveline.

B3-11 Mlle Camargo dancing to a pipe and drum. The design is adapted from Laurent Cars' engraving of Lancret's picture of the same subject (Wallace Coll.).

B3-12 A gentleman putting on a girl's skate. Sometimes found signed *J. Sadler*. The design is adapted from de Larmessin's engraving of Lancret's 'Winter'.

B3-12

B 4 - Genteel Society

B4–1

B4–2

B4-3

B4-1 A windy day, with a couple by the shore and a boatman. Sometimes found signed *Sadler*.

B4-2 A gentleman helping a girl over a stile. Sometimes found signed *Sadler*. The design is from a print by C. Moseley entitled 'Country prospect in calm'.

B4-3 'Miss Nancy Dawson dancing the Hornpipe'. This is the original title of the design, but it also occurs without a title in the *Ladies Amusement*, Plate 32 (Fig.3 on p.8). Sometimes found signed *J. Sadler Liverpool*. The same print was adapted by the delftware painters (Fig.8).

B4-4   B4-5   B4–6

B4–7   B4-8   B4–9

(Fig.8). Polychrome tinglazed plate painted with the scene of Miss Nancy Dawson dancing the Hornpipe copied from plate 32. *Ladies Amusement.* cf. *B4-3* and (Fig.3).

(Fig.9) A boy watching a girl blowing bubbles - from the John Bowles drawing book of 1756-7 (Norman Stretton Collection). Compare with *B4-8.*

B4-4   A lady and gentleman in tartans dancing. Sometimes found signed *J. Sadler Liverpool.*

B4-5   A gentleman standing playing the flute to a seated girl singing.

B4-6   Blind man's bluff. cf. the later design, *D4-13.*

B4-7   Two youths and a girl fishing. The design is adapted from the John Bowles drawing-book, Plate 32.

B4-8   A boy watching a girl blow bubbles. The design is from the John Bowles drawing-book, Plate 39, the sheet dated 1 January 1757 (Fig.9).

B4-9   Shuttlecock and battledore. Sometimes found signed *J. Sadler Liverpool.* cf. the later polychrome version, *C2-2.*

B 4 - Genteel Society (continued)

B4-10

B4-11

B4-12

B4-13

B4-14

B4-15

B4-10 A nursemaid with two children, one learning to walk. The design is taken from the John Bowles drawing-book, the sheet dated 23 November 1756. In simplified form it is also found on Liverpool painted titles (Ray, 1982, pl.79a).

B4-11 A lady and gentleman in a garden admiring an orange tree.

B4-12 A lady and gentleman in a garden with a pine-apple plant. The design is adapted from Plate 32 of the *Ladies Amusement*. cf. the later version, in reverse, *D4-11*.

B4-13 Two girls at a table drinking coffee, and a ?fortune-teller. Sometimes found signed *J. Sadler*.

B4-14 A tea-party with a negro boy holding a kettle.

B4-15 A tea-party, with a maid pouring from a kettle. The design is from the John Bowles drawing-book, the sheet dated 2 July 1757. cf. the polychrome version *C2-6*.

B5 - Street Scenes, (possibly after Hayman or Gravelot)

B5-1

B5-2

B5-1 'May-day', the chimney-sweep's annual celebration. Sometimes found signed *J. Sadler Liverpool*.

B5-2 A street-scene with a fiddler and a girl dancing. Sometimes found signed *J. Sadler Liverpool*.

B 6 - Rustic Life - Soldiers and Sailors

B6-1

B6-2

B6-3

B6-4

B6-5

B6-6

B6-7

B6-8

B6-9

B6-1   'The Tithe-pig'. Sometimes found signed *J. Sadler Liverp[1]*. The design is from an engraving by J. S. Müller after Boitard. Also found printed on useful wares (Fig.4).

B6-2   Huntsmen and a peasant couple, with a dead dog and bird.

B6-3   The overturned milk-pail; a girl rousing a sleeping boy. Sometimes found signed *J. Sadler Liverp[1]*.

B6-4   The see-saw.

B6-5   A scholar teaching a girl to sing. Sometimes found signed *J. Sadler Liverp[1]*.

B6-6   Rustic lovers by a windmill.

B6-7   Rustic lovers interrupted by an old woman. cf. the polychrome version, *C3-9*.

B6-8   A gallant and girl by a broken fence.

B6-9   A girl with a basket, and a fortune-teller with a baby on her back.

B6-10

B6-11

B6-12

B6-13

B6-14

B6-15

B6-16

B6-17

B6-18

B6-10 A peasant dancing to a fiddler outside an inn.

B6-11 A lad being apprehended outside an inn ('The Three Horse-shoes').

B6-12 A family skating, the woman with a bundle on her head; the design is adapted from Thomas Major's engraving of 'Winter' by Paul Ferg, 1754.

B6-13 A peasant couple dancing in a field.

B6-14 A woman churning butter, and a boy. The design, from Plate 45 of the John Bowles drawing-book, is also common on Liverpool painted tiles (Ray, 1973b., pl.28g).

B6-15 Two peasants picknicking, and a girl holding a hay-rake. cf. the polychrome version, *C3-4*.

B6-16 A farmyard with geese; a girl carrying a cage on her head. Sometimes found signed J. *Sadler.*

B6-17 A girl carrying a cloak and basket, and a pedlar with a pack resting under a tree.

B6-18 A peasant having a tooth extracted. The design is taken from an engraving entitled 'Feeling', one of the five senses, by Jan Both after Andries Both (Watney, 1987, pl.49).

B6-19   B6-20   B6-21

B6-22   B6-23

B6-19   The baby's toilet. The design is taken from an engraving entitled 'Smelling', one of the five senses, by Jan Both after Andries Both (Watney, 1987, pl.53).

B6-20   'The Sailor's Farewell' - 1.

B6-21   'The Sailor's Return' - 1. cf. the early version, *A2-2*, which shows the 'Lion of Scotland' rather than the 'King of Prussia'.

B6-22   'The Sailor's Farewell' - 2. The design is also found printed on delftware plates. cf. the polychrome version, *C3-7*.

B6-23   'The Sailor's Return' - 2. The design is derived from an engraving with this title by T. Booth after Boitard, 1744.

B 7 - Chinoiserie Scenes

B7-1   A Chinese woman fishing accompanied by a boy. Sometimes found signed *Sadler Liverpool.*

B7-2   A Chinaman with an umbrella, a woman holding a macaw, and a child.

B7-1   B7-2

B 8 - Ruins

B8-1

B8-2

B8-3

B8-4

B8-5

B8-6

B8-7

B8-8

B8-1 A ruined portico and a bridge and tower on a river. Sometimes found signed *J. Sadler Liverpool*. Part of this design is found, in reverse, on a later tile, *D7-1*.

B8-2 A three-arch bridge with a temple and a tree.

B8-3 Trajan's Column with the Temple of Castor. The design incorporates elements from Pannini (Handley, 1982).

B8-4 Ruined columns and arches with an obelisk beyond.

B8-5 A ruined portico with female figures, and a mausoleum behind. The design incorporates elements from Pannini (Handley, 1982).

B8-6 Ruins overgrown with vegetation: two figures, one reclining.

B8-7 Ruins overgrown with vegetation: a man seated with a stick.

B8-8 Ruins overgrown with vegetation: a man sketching.

B 9 - Ships

B9-1

B9-2

B9-3

B9-4

B9-5

B9-6

B9-7

B9-8

B9-9

B9-1   A ship seen inside a rocky grotto. Sometimes found signed *J. Sadler Liverp[1]*.

B9-2   A ship seen from the starboard bow under full sail in a choppy sea. Sometimes found signed *Sadler Liverpool*, in which version it also appears on a Liverpool porcelain coffee-pot of c.1756, but presumably printed in the 1760s (Watney, 1987, pl.52).

B9-3   A ship seen from the starboard bow, becalmed.

B9-4   A ship seen from the starboard quarter, tacking to port. One example is signed *Sadler C Liverp[1]*.

B9-5   A ship seen from the starboard quarter, firing a gun.

B9-6   A ship seen from the port quarter, tacking to starboard; a second ship in the distance.

B9-7   A ship seen from the starboard quarter, with jib set.

B9-8   A ship seen from the port beam. The design is very close to those on Liverpool ship-bowls.

B9-9   A ship seen from the port beam; a flag on the bow-sprit.

B 9 - Ships (continued)

B9-10

B9-10 A ship seen from the port bow, with a smaller vessel beyond. Signed *Sadler Co. Liverp[1]*

C - TILES PRINTED WITHOUT A BORDER ?1765 - 1770

C-1 Ships, (mostly printed in bluish grey.)

C1-1 A pilot-vessel seen from the starboard beam.
C1-2 A two-master seen from the port beam.
C1-3 A ship seen from the port beam, with jib set.
C1-4 A ship seen from the port beam; St George's flag aft.
C1-5 A schooner seen from the port quarter.
C1-6 A pilot-cutter, and a schooner seen from the starboard bow.
C1-7 A ship under full sail seen from the port beam, and a smaller ship.

C1-1

C1-2

C1-3

C1-4

C1-5

C1-6

C1-7

C 2 - Genteel Life - (printed in black and enamelled in colours)

C2-1

C2-2

C2-3

C2-4

C2-5

C2-6

C2-1   A gallant and lady by a stile. The design, which is also found printed on Bow porcelain, comes from *Clio and Euterpe* Vol.1 (1758), p.149 (see *Trans E.C.C.*, Vol. 2, 1948, Pl. XCIII).

C2-2   Shuttlecock and battledore. cf. the earlier monochrome version, *B4-9*.

C2-3   A man playing the flute and a girl singing. The design, which is also found in painted versions (Ray, 1973a, No. 218), comes from the John Bowles drawing-book, the sheet dated 24 November 1756 (Fig.10).

C2-4   A nursemaid brushing a boy's hat. cf. the later version, *D4-12*. Both are adapted from Lépicié's engraving (1739) of Chardin's painting 'La Gouvernante', of 1738.

C2-5   A gentleman holding a glass, with a negro boy putting on his boot.

C2-6   A tea-party, with a maid pouring from a kettle. cf. the earlier version *B4-15*.

(Fig.10)

(Fig.10). A man playing the flute and a girl singing (cf. *C2-3*) (Norman Stretton Collection).
- from the John Bowles drawing-book of 1756-7.

C 3 - Rustic Life, Sailors - (printed in black and enamelled in colours)

C3-1

C3-2

C3-3

C3-4

C3-5

C3-6

C3-7

C3-8

C3-9

C3-1   A gallant and shepherdess. Variants of the design are found on other Liverpool wares.

C3-2   A shepherd courting a shepherdess. cf. the later version, *D5-1*.

C3-3   A huntsman with a dog and a dead hare.

C3-4   A peasant with a barrel and a girl with a rake: a goat to the right. cf. the earlier design with a third figure instead of the goat, *B6-15*.

C3-5   'Harvest Home', The design corresponds with an engraving with this title by June after Grimm, but it is also found in *Clio and Euterpe*, Vol. 1, p.176, in reverse. A different version is found on creamware and mentioned in a letter to Wedgwood, 27th March 1763 (Stretton, 1970).

C3-6   The fortune-teller. cf. the later version. *D5-15*. Both from the John Bowles drawing-book, the sheet dated 24 November 1756 (Fig.11), but here omitting two figures.

C3-7   'The Sailor's Farewell'. cf. the earlier version, *B6-22*.

C3-8   The astrologer. cf. the later version, *D3-9*.

C3-9   Rustic lovers interrupted by an old woman. cf. the earlier version. *B6-7*.

C 4 - Literary Sources - (printed in black and enamelled in colours)

C4-1

C4-2

C4-1 'The Blind Carrying the Lame'. cf. the later design, *D3-8*. The source is Dodsley's Select Fables of Aesop and other Fabulists, the edition published by Osborne and Moseley in about 1764-5.

C4-2 Harlequin and Columbine surprised by Pierrot. cf. the later version, D2-3 (in reverse). The design is from the John Bowles drawing-book (Fig.1).

C 5 - Oriental Subjects - (printed in black and enamelled in colours)

C5-1

C5-2

C5-1 Chinese figures with a chime of bells. cf. the later version, *D6-2*. Both are derived from the *Ladies Amusement*, Plate 43.

C5-2 The Turkish merchant. cf. the later version, *D6-1*.

(Fig.11)

(Fig.11) The fortune-teller (cf. *C3-6* and *D5-15*) - from the John Bowles drawing-book of 1756-7.

D - LATER DESIGNS WITH THE '88' BORDER ?1765 - c.1775

D - 1 - Religious Subjects

D1-1

D1-2

D1-3

D1-4

D1-1   Abraham and Isaac.

D1-2   David with the head of Goliath.

D1-3   The return of the Prodigal Son. The same plate was used for printing
on creamware: cf. the Wedgwood plate in the Schreiber Collection,
Vol. II, No. 401 l. which has an enamelled swag border linking it to the
Fable plates (see heading to section *D-8*).

D1-4   Christ and the woman of Samaria. The design is from an engraving by
Carlo Maratta after Annibale Carracci (*Trans. E.C.C.*, Vol. 5, Pt. 2,
Plate 79).

D 2 - Scenes from Art, Literature and the Theatre

D2-1

D2-2

D2-3

D2-1   'Mercury instructing Cupid before Venus.' The design is ultimately derived from Correggio's 'School of Love',
now in the National Gallery, London.

D2-2   A scene from a play, perhaps from a Garrick comedy, although it has been called 'Le Malade Imaginaire'.

D2-3   Harlequin and Columbine surprised by Pierrot. The design, versions of which are found on creamware and
porcelain, is evidently taken from the John Bowles drawing-book, the sheet dated 24 November 1756 (Fig.1).

D2-4

D2-5

D2-6

D2-7

D2-8

D2-4   Harlequin between ?Ragonda and Columbine. There may be some connection with the theatrical tile, *F1-16*.

D2-5   Figures in medieval costume.

D2-6   A boy carrying hats, and a girl; a windy day. Watson (*Connoisseur*, Vol. LXX, 1924) links the words on the house 'A Lecture on Heads' with a song of this title composed by George Stevens, a well-known habitué of the Cider Cellar in Mincing Lane.

D2-7   The disguised astrologer. A theatrical scene; the astrologer appears to be a woman in disguise.

D2-8   'Don Quixote renouncing chivalry.' The design, called 'An allegory of the French Revolution' by Watson, 1927, is close to engraved scenes depicting Don Quixote released from folly by a figure representing Wisdom.

D 3 - Satirical and Moral Subjects

D3-1

D3-2

D3-3

D3-4

D3-5

D3-6

D3-7

D3-8

D3-9

D3-1   'The Pluralist and the Old Soldier.' The design satirises the wealth of the Church, symbolised by Lincoln Cathedral. The design is from T. Bobbin's *The Human Passions Delineated*, this scene dated 1770.

D3-2   'A Macaroni at a Sale of Pictures'. The design is from a print after Brandoin. The 'catalogue' is of pictures by Bar(-tolozzi).

D3-3   'The Little Marquis and his Valet.' The design is from a picture called 'Le Petit Maître et son Valet' by Brandoin.

D3-4   'A Six Weeks Tour to Paris'. The design is from an engraving by Caldwell of a picture by John Collet called 'L'Anglois à Paris', 10 May 1770.

D3-5   The English Cook. This design and *D3-6* come from a double print of 1772 by Brandoin entitled 'France. England'. The two cooks are contrasted: the English Cook is well fed -

D3-6   The French Cook is skinny and resorts to eating cats and frogs.

D3-7   The Fable of the Sticks. The design does not form part of the main Fable series (*D8*), and is probably earlier.

D3-8   'The Blind Carrying the Lame'. cf. the polychrome version, *C4-1*. Variants of the design, from Dodsley's *Fables*, occur on creamware.

D3-9   The astrologer. The fortunate girl has a scroll inscribed 'A brisk husband soon': the unfortunate girl has one inscribed 'Never to be married'. Variants are found on creamware. cf. The polychrome version, *C3-8*.

D 4 - Scenes from Genteel Life

D4-1

D4-2

D4-3

D4-4

D4-5

D4-6

(Fig.12) A print by Wiliam Woollett showing the canal and *Gothick* folly in the garden of The Third Duke of Argyll at Whitton. The tile-design (*D4-2*) copies the building and two of the figures on the left.

(Fig.13) A sheet from the John Bowles drawing book dated 2 July 1757 (*D4-5*).

D4-1   A gentleman doffing his hat to two ladies. The design comes from the *Ladies' Amusement*, Pl. 28. A fragment in the Liverpool Museum shows that the design also occurred on painted tiles.

D4-2   A lady and gentleman by a *Gothick* folly. The design is adapted from a print by W. Woollett, of June 1757, showing the canal and folly in the garden of the Third Duke of Argyll at Whitton (Fig.11).

D4-3   A gentleman with two ladies; a cascade in the distance.

D4-4   A suitor offering a present to a girl.

D4-5   A lady and gentleman on a seat, with a child playing. The design comes from the John Bowles drawing-book, the sheet dated 2 July 1757 (Fig.13).

D4-6   An old lady in a chair, with two gentlemen.

D4-7

D4-8

D4-9

D4-10

D4-11

D4-12

D4-13

D4-14

D4-7   A cleric and two gentlemen drinking at a table.
D4-8   A lady by a seat, with tall trees behind and a maid with a dog in the background.
D4-9   Three ladies by a fountain.
D4-10   A lady and gentleman dancing to a fiddler; an obelisk in the background.
D4-11   A couple in a garden with a pine-apple plant. cf. the earlier version, in reverse, *B4-12.*
D4-12   A nursemaid brushing a boy's hat; after Chardin. cf. the polychrome version, *C2-4.*
D4-13   Blind man's bluff. The second design with this subject. cf. *B4-6.*
D4-14   Three girls teasing a dog.

D 4 - Scenes from Genteel Life (continued)

D4-15

D4-15a

D4-15 Two sportsmen with guns and dogs. The design goes back to Stubbs's painting of 1766-7 showing 'Two Gentlemen shooting at Cresswell Crags' (Taylor, *Stubbs*, Pl. 48), but the immediate source is an engraving of this picture by W. Woollett published on 1 August 1769 by Thomas Bradford as the first of four shooting scenes. The tree is Woollett's invention.

D4-15a The same scene but in reverse.

D 5 - Scenes from Rustic Life

D5-1

D5-2

D5-3

D5-1 A shepherd courting a shepherdess. cf. the polychrome version, *C3-2*.

D5-2 A gallant and shepherdess, and an old woman wringing her hands. The design is after Boitard (Cook, *Robert Hancock*, Item 99).

D5-3 A gallant and country lass, and a man with a stick climbing a stile. Variants of this design are found on creamware.

D 5 - Scenes from Rustic Life (continued)

D5-4

D5-5

D5-6

D5-7

D5-8

D5-9

D5-10

D5-11

D5-12

D5-4   A gallant chucking a country lass under the chin, watched by a boy.

D5-5   A rustic couple courting, with the unsuccessful suitor going off in despair.

D5-6   A man kneeling on a bench with his hand on a girl's shoulder; she is singing, evidently accompanied by a seated fiddler. (The illustration is unreliable in the detail, since it is a touched up print of a poor photograph.)

D5-7   A peasant offering a bird cage to a girl.

D5-8   A sailor offering a present to a country lass, watched by a peasant. The design is from the *Ladies' Amusement*, Pl.33.

D5-9   A peasant with a gun and dog, and a girl holding out her apron.

D5-10 A rustic couple with a baby and cradle outside a cottage. The design is from the John Bowles drawing-book (Fig.14a).

D5-11 A one-legged fiddler outside an inn, with a dog begging and three children watching.

D5-12 Two children dancing to a flute-player, watched by a woman.

D 5 - Scenes from Rustic Life (continued)

(Fig.14 a & b)
Two scenes from
the John Bowles
drawing book.
From a sheet dated
24 November 1756
(*D5-10*) (*D5-13*).

(Fig.14 a).

(Fig.14 b).

D5-13

D5-14

D5-15

D5-16

D5-17

D5-18

D5-13 A peasant woman escorting a drunken man home. The design is from the John Bowles drawing-book, the sheet dated 24 November 1756 (Fig.14b).

D5-14 A drunken peasant waving his hat, escorted home by a woman and a boy holding a whip. The design is from an engraving by F. Van Reysschoot of Teniers' picture 'The Happy Man' (Watney, 1972).

D5-15 A fortune-teller and a girl with a rake. cf. the polychrome version, *C3-6* and (Fig.15). Variants of the design are found on creamware.

D5-16 A one-legged beggar and his companion singing ballads.

D5-17 Itinerant musicians, with barrel-organ, hurdy-gurdy and triangle.

D5-18 A child on stilts in a cloak and wig with other children beating a drum and waving a flag.

D5-19

D5-20

D5-21

D5-22

D5-23

D5-24

D5-19 The village school.

D5-20 A pipe and punch party. Variants of the design are found on creamware.

D5-21 Four peasants carousing outside a tavern, served by a maid.

D5-22 Three peasants carousing at a table.

D5-23 Five peasants carousing, one holding up a glass. Versions in relief are found on Herculaneum pottery and Prattware (see Alan Smith, *Trans. E.C.C.*, Vol. 7, Pt. I, Pl. 19). From an engraving by Mercier after Teniers (Fig.15).

D5-24 A girl with a hurdy-gurdy.

(Fig.15)
Engraving of Peasants drinking 1730-40.
An engraving by Philip Mercier (1689-1760)
after a painting by David Teniers the
Younger (1610-90). (Trustees of the British
Museum)

D5-25   D5-26   D5-27

D5-25 'A Modern Demi-rep on the Look-out.' The design, which also occurs on creamware, is from a print of this title by Grignion after Brandoin, published by Sayer, 25 September 1771 (Fig.16).

D5-26 'An Opera Girl of Paris in the Character of Flora'. The design, which also occurs on creamware, is from a print of this title by Grignion after Brandoin, published by Sayer, 1 December 1771 (Fig.17).

D5-27 'The Pretty Mantua-maker.' The design is from a print of this title by Grignion after Brandoin, published by Sayer in 1772.

(Fig.16) A print by Grignion after Brandoin, published by Sayer 25 Sept 1771.

(Fig.17) A print by Grignion after Brandoin, published by Sayer 1st Dec 1771.

D 6 - Oriental Subjects

D6-1

D6-2

D6-3

D6-1   The Turkish merchant. The same design is found on Wedgwood creamware. cf. the polychrome version *C5-2*.

D6-2   Two Chinese figures playing a chime of bells watched by two children. cf. the polychrome version, *C5-1*.

D6-3   Three Chinese figures, with the boy peering through what looks like a letter of a *chinoiserie* alphabet. The design, which is sometimes found signed 'Green', is taken from a plate in Pillement's *Petits Parasols Chinois*, published in 1774.

D 7 - Ruins

D7-1

D7-1   A bridge and tower by an estuary, with boatmen and a man with a dog. This is part of the earlier ruin design, *B8-1*, but in reverse.

D 8 - Aesop's Fables

The following forty five designs all occur in Croxall's edition (*Cr.*):(cf. Fig.18). Two other fable subjects from different sources are listed above, *D3-7* and *D3-8*. The designs marked with an * are also found on the set of creamware plates printed in red and with green enamelled borders in the Victoria and Albert Museum (Schreiber Collection - Vol. II, No. 401) and in the British Museum.

D8-1   D8-2   D8-3

D8-4   D8-5   D8-6

D8-7   D8-8   D8-9

*D8-1**   The angler and the little fish : *Cr–LXXI*.
*D8-2**   The ape and the fox: *Cr–CXXIII*.
D8-3   The bear and the bee-hives: *Cr–CXXVI*.
*D8-4**   The hunted beaver: *Cr–LXII*.
D8-5   The boar and the ass: *Cr–XIV*.
D8-6   The cat and the fox: *Cr–LX*.
*D8-7**   The cock in the tree and the fox: *Cr– CXXVII*.
D8-8   The cock and the fox caught in a trap: *Cr–CXCIII*.
D8-9   The crow and the pitcher: *Cr–LIII*.

D8-10

D8-11

D8-12

D8-13

D8-14

D8-15

D8-16

D8-17

D8-18

D8-10   The deer and the lion: *Cr–CXCI.*
*D8-11**   The one-eyed doe: *Cr–XCIX.*
D8-12   The dog in the manger: *Cr–CXXIX.*
D8-13   The mischievous dog: *Cr–XLIV.*
D8-14   The dog and the shadow: *Cr–V.*
*D8-15**   The dog and the sheep: *Cr–CXXX.*
D8-16   The dog and the wolf: *Cr–XIX.*
D8-17   The fowler and the ring-dove: *Cr–CLII.*
D8-18   The fox and the ass: *Cr–CLXXVIII.*

D8-19   D8-20   D8-21

D8-22   D8-23   D8-24

D8-25   D8-26   D8-27

D8-19   The fox and the boar: *Cr–XCV.*
D8-20   The fox and the crow: *Cr–IX.*
D8-21   The fox and the lion: *Cr–CXXXVI.*
D8-22   The fox and the stork: *Cr–XII.*
D8-23* The fox and the tiger: *Cr–LI.*
D8-24* The fox in the well: *Cr–CLXVI.*
D8-25   The geese and cranes: *Cr–CXXXVII.*
D8-26   The hare and the tortoise: *Cr–CLIX.*
D8-27   The hares and the frogs: *Cr–XXX.*

D 8 - Aesop's Fables (continued)

D8-28

D8-29

D8-30

D8-31

D8-32

D8-33

D8-34

D8-35

D8-36

*D8-28** The hawk and the farmer: *Cr–CXXXI.*
*D8-29** The jackdaw and the sheep: *Cr–CLXXXIV.*
D8-30 The lamb brought up by a goat: *Cr–XX.*
*D8-31** The lark and her young ones: *Cr–XXXVIII.*
D8-32 The lion and the frog: *Cr–LXXXII.*
*D8-33** The lioness and the fox: *Cr–LXVIII.*
*D8-34** Mercury and the woodman: *Cr–CXI.*
*D8-35** The old hound: *Cr–XXVIII.*
D8-36 The owl and the grasshopper: *Cr–XCVIII.*

D8-37

D8-38

D8-39

D8-40

D8-41

D8-42

D8-43

D8-44

D8-45

D8-37 The sheepbiter: *Cr–CVI.*

D8-38 The sow and the bitch: *Cr–CIII.*

D8-39 The sow and the wolf: *Cr–CLIII.*

D8-40 The stag looking into the water: *Cr–VIII.*

D8-41 The stag and the fawn: *Cr–LXIX.*

D8-42 The two travellers and the bear: *Cr–XLVI.*

D8-43* The wolf and the lamb: *Cr–XXXIII.* This design, which is the only one which differs appreciably from that in Croxall, is clearly based on an engraving by Sebastien Leclerc.

D8-44 The wood and the clown: *Cr–XXXIII.*

D8-45 The young man and the swallow: *Cr–LXX.* cf.(Fig.18).

(Fig.18) An illustration from Croxall's edition of Aesop's Fables (*D8-45*).

NEO - CLASSICAL DESIGNS, c. 1770 - 1780

E 1 - Figure Subjects (these tiles are printed in black and enamelled in green).

E1-1

E1-2

E1-3

E1-4

E1-5

E1-6a

E1-1   Hercules between Vice and Virtue. The design and ribbon-tie must derive from the Wedgwood and Bentley plaque with this subject (Fig.20).

E1-2   Neptune.

E1-3   Diana (from *Polymetis*, Pl. XIV-II - 'Diana Celestis; a statue at the Earl of Leicester's House in London').

E1-4   Mercury (from *Polymetis*, Pl. XIV-IV - 'Mercury; a statue in the Great Duke's Collection, at Florence').

E1-5   Bacchus (from *Polymetis*, Pl. XX-I - 'Bacchus; a statue at the Marquis Cavalieri's, in Rome').

E1-5a   Bacchus: green ground (*Horne*, Cat No. 334g).

E1-6   Apollo: white ground (from the *1749 Horace*, pl. 8 - 'Apollo Musicus': also found in *Polymetis*, described as 'from a known medal of Adrian') (Fig.19a).

E1-6a   Apollo: green ground (*Horne*, Cat No. 334a).

(Fig.19 a)

(Fig.19 b)

(Fig.19 a & b)

Engravings by J. S. Müller illustrating an edition of *Horace*, published by William Sandby in 1749; the designs being mostly taken from Antique gems, coins and other objects.
(Fig. a) Apollo (cf. *E1-6*).
(Fig. b) Fortune (cf. *E1-8*).

E 1 - Neo-classical designs, c.1770 - 1780 (continued)

E1-7

E1-8

E1-9a

E1-10

E1-11

E1-12

E1-7 A Muse with a lyre; white ground (from the *1749 Horace*, pl.2 - 'Musa Lyram Tractans').

E1-7a A Muse; green ground (*Horne*, Cat No. 334c).

E1-8 Fortune; green ground (from the *1749 Horace*, pl.18 - 'Fortuna Manens'; also in *Polymetis*, described as 'from a common medal of Adrian') (Fig:19b).

E1-9 The Three Graces; white ground (from the *1749 Horace*, pl.14 - 'Gratiae cum Vasis Vinariis'; also in *Polymetis*, described as 'from a sepulchral lamp that formerly belonged to P. S. Bartoli').

E1-9a The Three Graces; green ground.

E1-10 The Four Seasons; white ground (from the *1749 Horace*, pl.22. For the ribbon-tie cf. *E1-1*).

E1-10a The Four Seasons; green ground.

E1-11 Cupid on a dolphin.

E1-12 Four ladies in classical costume; for the ribbon-tie cf. *E1-1*.

E1-12a Four ladies in classical costume; green ground (*Horne*, Cat No. 334f).

E1-13 Four ladies in classical costume; one playing a tambourine.

E1-13

(Fig.20)
A Wedgwood and Bentley plaque of 1777 depicting 'Hercules between Vice and Virtue'. The tile-design (*E1-1*) not only copies the figures but also the Birmingham ormolu mount. (Courtesy of the Trustees of the Wedgwood Museum, Barlaston)

(Fig.20)

E 2 - Vases and Urns with a heavy Border

E2-1

E2-2

E2-3

E2-4

E2-5

E2-6

E2-7

E2-8

E2-9

E2-1   Ewer with swags springing from a mask.
E2-2   Vase with dolphin neck and a wreath with crossed tridents (Darly, pl.42).
E2-3   Ewer with the figure of a nymph and child; the handle with dolphin masks.
E2-4   Urn with snake handles and masks.
E2-5   Vase of elaborate shape with a garland of flowers, and cover with floral knop.
E2-6   Urn with fretted handles and a draped swag.
E2-7   Tall-necked urn with masks, medallions and swags.
E2-8   Lidded urn with three portrait medallions between swags (Darly, pl.37; cover added).
E2-9   Tall urn with ribbon and garland swags (Darly, pl.7).

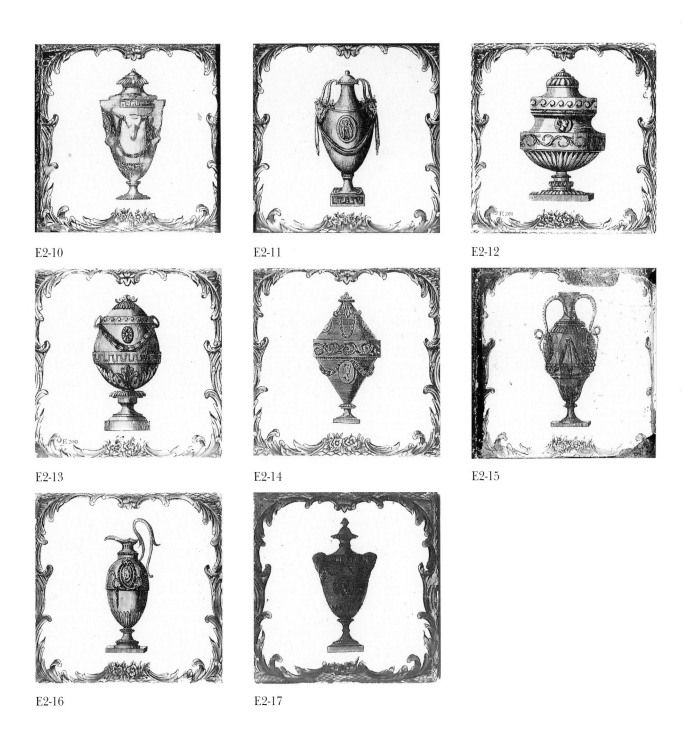

E2-10

E2-11

E2-12

E2-13

E2-14

E2-15

E2-16

E2-17

E2-10 Covered urn with goat's head and swags (Darly, pl.43, adapted).

E2-11 Urn with a medallion and satyr-mask handles.

E2-12 Covered urn with acanthus scrolls and a portrait medallion (Darly, pl.25, adapted).

E2-13 Ovoid urn with a medallion and swag; acanthus base (Darly, pl.11).

E2-14 Vase of lozenge shape with an acanthus scroll and portrait medallion (Darly, pl.24; a combination of two vases).

E2-15 Tall urn on a high foot with snake handles and swags (Darly, pl.20; handles cdded).

E2-16 Ewer with a portrait medallion (Darly, pl.34).

E2-17 Urn with mask handles and a female portrait medallion.

E 3 - Urns and Vessels with simple Borders

E3-1

E3-2

E3-3

E3-4

E3-5

E3-6

E3-7

E3-8

E3-1   Covered bowl in a circle border; florettes in the corners. The design does not fit precisely into either Section 2 or 3, but in style it is closer to those in Section 3.

E3-2   Urn with dolphin neck and a wreath with crossed tridents. The design is based on *E2-2*.

E3-3   Ovoid urn with a medallion and wreath; acanthus base. The design is based on *E2-13*.

E3-4   Urn with ram's head and swags. The design is apparently based on *E2-10*.

E3-5   Ovoid urn with a mask and swags; human head pedestal.

E3-6   Urn with dolphin handles.

E3-7   Urn with florette medallion and swags.

E3-8   Urn with elaborate handles and a mask.

F - THEATRICAL c.1777 - 1780
F 1 - Heavy Borders, probably printed by Green.

F1-1

F1-2

F1-3

F1-4

F1-5

F1-6

F1-1   'Mrs Abbington in the Character of Estifania' in Beaumont and Fletcher's *Rule a Wife and Have a Wife*. The print, from Bell's *British Theatre*, is simply signed 'Roberts del.' and dated 20 May 1776.

F1-2   'Mrs Barry in the Character of Athenais' in Nathaniel Lee's *Theodosius*. The print, from Bell's *British Theatre*, is by Thornthwaite after Roberts and dated 12 December 1776.

F1-3   'Mrs Barry in the Character of Sir Harry Wildair' in Farquhar's *The Constant Couple*. The print, from Lowndes' *New English Theatre*, is by Goldar after Dodd and dated 17 May 1777.

F1-4   'Mr Bensley in the Character of Mahomet' in Miller's *Mahomet*. The print, from Bell's *British Theatre*, is by Thornthwaite after Roberts and dated 1 December 1776.

F1-5   'Mrs Bulkeley in the Character of Angelina' in Colley Cibber's *Love makes a Man*. The print, from Bell's *British Theatre*, is by Thornthwaite after Roberts and dated 20 October 1776.

F1-6   'Mrs Cibber in the Character of Monimia' in Otway's *The Orphan*. The print, from Bell's *British Theatre*, is by Thornthwaite 'from a picture in the possession of D. Garrick Esq.' and dated 1 September 1776.

F1-7

F1-8

F1-9

F1-10

F1-11

F1-12

F1-7 'Mr Foote in the Character of Fondlewife' in Congreve's *The Old Batchelor*. The print, from Bell's *British Theatre*, is by Thornthwaite after Roberts and dated 4 June 1776.

F1-8 'Mr Garrick in the Character of Abel Drugger' in Jonson's *The Alchemist*. The print is from Sayer's *Dramatic Characters*, published in 1770.

F1-9 'Mr Garrick in the Character of Sir John Brute' in Vanbrugh's *The Provoked Wife*. The print, from Lowndes' *New English Theatre*, is by I. Taylor and dated 1776.

F1-10 'Mr Garrick in the Character of Don John in the Chances' - the play by Beaumont and Fletcher. The print, from Lowndes' *New English Theatre*, is by Hall after Loutherbourg and dated 1777.

F1-11 'Mrs Hartley as Lady Jane Grey' in Rowe's tragedy with that title. The print, from Bell's *British Theatre*, is by Page after Roberts and dated 26 December 1776.

F1-12 'Mrs Hartley in the Character of Imoinda' in Southerne's *Oroonoko*. The print, from Bell's *British Theatre*, is by Thornthwaite after Roberts and dated 1 March 1777.

F1-13   F1-14   F1-15

F1-16   F1-17   F1-18

F1-13   'Miss P. Hopkins in the Character of Lavinia' in Shakespeare's *Titus Andronicus*. The print, from Bell's *Shakespeare*, is simply signed 'J. Roberts del.' and dated 6 March 1776.

F1-14   'Mr King in the Character of Lissardo' in Mrs Centlivre's *The Wonder*. The print, from Bell's *British Theatre*, is by Ja. Roberts after J. Roberts and dated 10 August 1776.

F1-15   'Mrs Lessingham in the Character of Ophelia' in Shakespeare's *Hamlet*. The print, from Bell's *Shakespeare*, is by Grignion after Roberts and dated 1 October 1775.

F1-16   'Mr Lee Lewis in the Character of Harlequin.' Charles (Lee) Lewis played Harlequin in *Harlequin's Invasion* at Drury Lane in 1759, the dialogue of the play being by Garrick. The print of this design is at present untraced, but it may be related to an anonymous and undated print in the Burney Collection of Theatrical Portraits in the British Museum, depicting 'Mr Lee Lewis speaking a prologue in the character of Harlequin'. See also *D2-4* and *F1-24*.

F1-17   'Mr Lee Lewis in the Character of Harlequin.' Like *F1-16* this design is from an untraced print.

F1-18   'Mr Lee Lewis in the Character of Sir Peter Teazle' in Sheridan's *School for Scandal;* source untraced.

F1-19   F1-20   F1-21

F1-22   F1-23   F1-24

F1-19   'Mr Lewis in the Character of Douglas' in Home's *Douglas*. The print, from Lowndes' *New English Theatre*, is by Goldar after Dodd and dated 21 June 1777. The actor is William Thomas Lewis.

F1-20   'Mr Lewis in the Character of Hippolytus' in Smith's *Phaedra and Hippolytus*. The print, from Lowndes' *New English Theatre*, is by Grignion after Dodd and dated 27 July 1776. The actor is William Thomas Lewis.

F1-21   'Mr Macklin in the Character of Shylock' in Shakespeare's *Merchant of Venice*. The print, from Bell's *Shakespeare*, is by Grignion after Parkinson and dated 20 November 1775.

F1-22   'Mr Macklin in the Character of Sr Gilbert Wrangle' in Colley Cibber's *The Refusal*. The print, from Bell's *British Theatre*, is by Thornthwaite after Roberts and dated 5 April 1777.

F1-23   'Mrs Mattocks as Prinˢ Catherine' in Shakespeare's *Henry V*. The print, from Bell's *Shakespeare*, is by Grignion after Roberts and dated 1 December 1775.

F1-24   'Mr Moody as Simon in Harlequin's Invasion.' For the play see *F1-16*. The anonymous print was published by J. Smith and R. Sayer in 1769.

F1-25

F1-26

F1-27

F1-28

F1-29

F1-30

F1-25 'Mr Moody in the Character of Teague' in Howard's *The Committee*. The print, from Bell's *British Theatre*, is by Waller after Roberts and dated 1 July 1776.

F1-26 'Mr Shuter in the Character of Lovegold' in Fielding's *The Miser*. The print, from Bell's *British Theatre*, is by Ja. Roberts after J. Roberts and dated 20 October 1776.

F1-27 'Mr Smith in the Character of Ld Townley' in Vanbrugh's *The Provoked Husband*. The print, from Bell's *British Theatre*, is by Thornthwaite after Roberts and dated 24 November 1776. See also *F1-35*.

F1-28 'Mr Ward in the Character of Rodogune' in Rowe's *The Royal Convert*. The anonymous print, from Bell's *British Theatre*, is after Roberts and dated November 1777.

F1-29 'Mr Wilson in the Character of Old Mirabel' in Farquhar's *The Inconstant*. The print, from Lowndes' *New English Theatre*, is by Goldar after Dodd and dated 3 May 1777.

F1-30 'Mr Woodward in the Character of Petruchio' in *Catherine and Petruchio*, Garrick's version of Shakespeare's *The Taming of the Shrew*. The anonymous print, from Bell's *Shakespeare*, is dated 5 January 1775 (Fig.22).

F1-31   F1-32   F1-33

F1-34   F1-35   F1-36

F1-31 'Mr Woodward in the Character of Razor' in Murphy's *The Upholsterer*. The anonymous print was published by J. Smith and R. Sayer in 1769.

F1-32 'Mrs Wrighten in the Character of Peggy' in Allen Ramsey's *The Gentle Shepherd*. The print, from Bell's *British Theatre*, is by Thornthwaite after Roberts and dated 15 July 1776.

F1-33 'Mr Wroughton in the Character of Barnwell' in Lillo's *The History of George Barnwell*. The print, from Bell's *British Theatre*, is after Roberts and dated 26 September 1776 (Fig.23).

F1-34 'Mrs Yates in the Character of Jane Shore' in Rowe's tragedy with this title. The print, from Lowndes' *New English Theatre*, is by Collyer after Dodd and dated 2 September 1776 (Fig.21).

F1-35 'Mrs Yates as Lady Townley' in Vanbrugh's *The Provok'd Husband*. The print, from Bell's *British Theatre*, is by Thornthwaite after Roberts and dated 24 November 1776. See also *F1-27*.

F1-36 'Miss Younge in the Character of Zara' in Congreve's *The Mourning Bride*. The print, from Bell's *British Theatre*, is by Thornthwaite after Roberts and dated 15 July 1776 (Fig.24).

(Fig.21) Print from Lowndes' *New English Theatre* dated 2nd September 1776 (*F1-34*).

(Fig.22) An anonymous print from Bell's *Shakespeare* dated 5th January 1776 (*F1-30*).

(Fig.23) Print from Bell's *British Theatre* dated 26 September 1776 (*F1-33*).

(Fig.24) Print from Bell's *British Theatre* dated 15 July 1776 (*F1-36*).

F 2 - Theatrical, with swag borders, printed by Richard Abbey 1773 - ?1777

F2-1

F2-2

F2-3

F2-4

F2-5

F2-6

F2-1   'Mr Beard in the Character of Hawthorn in Love in Village Act I Scene 6th.' *Love in a Village* is a comic opera by
Isaac Bickerstaffe. The anonymous print, after a picture by Zoffany, was published by R. Sayer.

F2-2   'Mr Dibden in the Character of Mungo' in Bickerstaffe's comic opera *The Padlock*. The anonymous and
undated print was published by R. Sayer.

F2-3   'Mr Foote in the Character of the Doctor in The Devil upon Two Sticks' – the play was written by Foote himself.
The anonymous and undated print was published by R. Sayer. The tile is signed 'Abbey Liverpool'.

F2-4   'Mr Weston in the Character of Dr Last in The Devil upon Two Sticks' – (see *F2-3*). The anonymous and
undated print was published by J. Smith and R. Sayer.

F2-5   'Mr Wilson in the Character of the Miser Act 4th scene last', in Fielding's *'The Miser'* (cf. *F1-26*).

F2-6   'Mrs Yates in the Character of Lady Macbeth,'in Shakespeare's *Macbeth* (Courtesy of the Detroit Institute of Arts).

G - MISCELLANEOUS POTTERY TILES, G1 - Overall Designs

G1-1

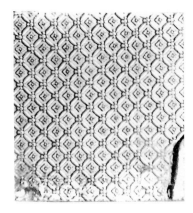

G1-2

G1-1 Flower heads printed in black and enamelled in green. Painted tiles with this pattern are known.

G1-2 A diaper pattern. This kind of pattern is common on the Liverpool clock-faces of the period.

G 2 - Border Tiles

G2-1

G2-2

G2-3

G2-4

G2-5

G2-1 A small octagonal panel depicting the fable of the 'Fox without a Tail', set in elaborate scrolls springing from a mask at the bottom of the tile, and two festoons of flowers held by a winged Cupid standing at the top. The design is adapted from a plate in Dodsley's *Select Fables of Aesop and other Fabulists*, Third Edition (1762), where, however, the fable in the centre is 'Death and Cupid'.

G2-2 Candelabra ornament. These tiles were evidently made to frame the first group of theatrical tiles (*F1*).

G2-3 Acanthus and ribbon scroll, printed in black and enamelled in mauve, green and yellow.

G2-4 A running acanthus scroll, printed in black and enamelled over in green. Evidently made to frame the neo-classical tiles.

G2-5 Greek key pattern, printed in black and enamelled green. Like *G2-3*, made evidently to frame neo-classical tiles.

Select Bibliography

| BRIDGES, | 1978 | Daisy Wade Bridges, 'Sadler Tiles in Colonial America' (*Trans. ECC.*, Vol. 10, Part 3, 1978, pp 174-183). |

BRIDGES, 1978 Daisy Wade Bridges, 'Sadler Tiles in Colonial America' (*Trans. ECC.*, Vol. 10, Part 3, 1978, pp 174-183).

DRAKARD, 1992 David Drakard, *Printed English Pottery*, London, 1992.

GARNER, 1972 F. H. Garner and Michael Archer, *English Delftware* (2nd edition), 1972.

HANDLEY, 1989 Joseph Handley, 'Robert Hancock and G-P Pannini' (*Trans. ECC.*, Vol. 11, Part 2, 1982, pp. 99-101).

HORNE, 1989 Jonathan Horne, *English Tin-glazed Tiles,* London, 1989.

PRICE, 1948 E. Stanley Price, *John Sadler, a Liverpool Pottery Printer*, West Kirby, 1948.

RAY, 1973a Anthony Ray, *English Delftware Tiles*, London, 1973.

1973b Anthony Ray, 'Liverpool Printed Tiles' (*Trans. ECC.* Vol. 9, Part 1, 1973, pp. 36-66).

1974 Anthony Ray, 'Liverpool Printed Tiles - Some Further Notes' (*Trans. ECC.* Vol. 9, Part 2, 1974, pp. 190-2).

1982 Anthony Ray, 'Delftware Diversions' (*Trans. ECC.* Vol. 11, Part 2, 1982, pp.157-160).

1994a Anthony Ray, 'Liverpool Printed Tiles - some further comments and additions' (*Trans. ECC.* Vol. 15, Part 2, 1994, pp. 190-3).

1994b Anthony Ray, 'Staffordshire Tiles 1750-1840' (*Trans. ECC.* Vol. 15, Part 2, 1994).

SMITH 1970 Alan Smith, *Liverpool Herculaneum Pottery*, London 1970.

STRETTON 1970 Norman Stretton, 'Early Sadler Prints on Wedgwood Creamware' (*Proceedings of the Wedgwood society*, No. 8, 1970, pp. 225-231).

1981 Norman Stretton, 'Some Unrecorded Liverpool Printed Tiles' (*Trans. ECC.* Vol. 11, Part 1, 1981, pp. 36-8).

1994 Norman Stretton, 'Fable Subjects on English Pottery' (*Trans. ECC.* Vol. 15, Part 2, 1994, pp. 205 ff.).

WATNEY 1966 Bernard Watney and Robert Charleston 'Petitions for Patents concerning Porcelain, Glass and Enamels with special reference to Birmingham, 'The Great Toyshop of Europe' (*Trans. ECC.* Vol. 6, Part 2, 1966, pp. 57-123).

1972 Bernard Watney, 'Origins of some designs for English Ceramics of the Eighteenth Century', *Burlington Magazine*, December 1972.

1987 Bernard Watney, 'Some Liverpool printed tiles' (*Burlington Magazine*, No. 1010, May 1987, pp. 316 ff.).

1993 Bernard Watney, 'William Jackson of Liverpool' (*Trans. ECC.* Vol. 15, Part 1, 1993).

WATSON 1927 J.A.G. Watson, 'Some of the Less Known Liverpool Transfer Tiles', *Connoisseur*, May 1927.

WILLIAMS-WOOD 1981 Cyril Williams-Wood, *English Transfer-printed Pottery and Porcelain*, London, 1981.

WYMAN 1980 Colin Wyman, 'The early techniques of transfer-printing' (*Trans. ECC.* Vol. 10, Parts 4 and 5, pp. 187-200).

**Other specialist books on English Pottery are available
from Jonathan Horne Antiques Ltd.
(Member of the British Antique Dealers Association)
66c Kensington Church Street, London W8 4BY.
Tel. 071-221 5658   Fax. 071-792 3090.**

BACK COVER

A1-1	A2-4	A1-8	A2-3
B4-13	B6-4	B5-1	B6-3
D4-13	B9-1	D5-24	B3-4
B6-20	D4-7	B2-1	B6-22
E1-13	E3-6	E1-8	E2-5